T0147127

The INCLUSIVE LEADER

An Applied Approach to Diversity, Change, and Management

DR. AMINE AYAD *and* DR. EMAD RAHIM

BALBOA.
PRESS
A DIVISION OF HAY HOUSE

Balboa Press books may be ordered through booksellers or by contacting:

Balboa Press
A Division of Hay House
1663 Liberty Drive
Bloomington, IN 47403
www.balboapress.com.au
1 (877) 407-4847

Because of the dynamic nature of the Internet, any web addresses or links contained in this book may have changed since publication and may no longer be valid. The views expressed in this work are solely those of the author and do not necessarily reflect the views of the publisher, and the publisher hereby disclaims any responsibility for them.

The author of this book does not dispense medical advice or prescribe the use of any technique as a form of treatment for physical, emotional, or medical problems without the advice of a physician, either directly or indirectly. The intent of the author is only to offer information of a general nature to help you in your quest for emotional and spiritual well-being. In the event you use any of the information in this book for yourself, which is your constitutional right, the author and the publisher assume no responsibility for your actions.

Any people depicted in stock imagery provided by Thinkstock are models, and such images are being used for illustrative purposes only. Certain stock imagery © Thinkstock.

Print information available on the last page.

ISBN: 978-1-5043-0025-4 (sc)
ISBN: 978-1-5043-0026-1 (e)

Library of Congress Control Number: 2016901313

Balboa Press rev. date: 02/04/2016

Contents

Foreword

Like parents have done for generations, I watch my children at play and think about the world they will inherit. My grandfather, born in 1901, became a man in the roaring 20's and subsequently had to raise a family through The Great Depression. His parents never could have imagined his burden. Nor could they have predicted how long he would have to work to reach a point of prosperity. My own parents, children of that Depression period went on to raise a family in the middle of the cold war with Russia -- a time when they saw their son growing up in a world with an abundance of nuclear weapons ready for launch at the push of a button. Each generation brings unique challenges and opportunities, and we depend on the thought leaders of the day to help us both comprehend our current state, and then begin to see with greater clarity what's on the horizon. In their book, Leading Through Diversity: Transforming Managers into Effective Leaders, Drs. Amine Ayad and Emad Rahim provide us with some timeless lessons in leadership, change, and innovation while simultaneously developing their work with a key eye on how the steep slope of change today will ultimately reshape how leaders lead, both in contemporary times and in generations to come.

Today the topic of diversity is clearly more important than ever. With factors like greater levels of international mobility, the ascent of the international middle class, and the ability to connect with one another in so many ways thanks to technology, leading organizations today with an eye on our own perspectives of diversity is extremely important. In studying the scholars of leadership and management over the last fifty years, it is clear that while there has been a great deal of attention to issues in multiculturalism and diversity, the focus unfortunately has revolved around the development of tolerance instead of an appreciation of opportunity. Simply put, many of our leaders from previous generations found themselves in charge of largely homogeneous teams who, when faced with small amounts of diversity, were asked to learn to be tolerant, understanding, and accepting of these differences. Today, however, the best leaders have come to understand that diversity is a value that must be purposefully pursued and carefully nurtured. If groups, for example, do happen to be largely homogeneous, wise leaders today understand that reaching out and actively creating a more heterogeneous and diverse environment ultimately improves productivity and the capacity to learn, grow, and innovate. The authors of this book understand this dynamic and their work here helps leaders continue to embrace this more evolved notion of diversity and what it means to leadership and change.

In this book, Ayad and Emad also shed a light on the importance of leading in a fair, transparent, and socially responsible manner. Clearly businesses today that don't operate in transparent ways run the risk of being revealed and subsequently punished in the court of public opinion thanks to the geometric powers of social media. Leaders who don't understand the importance of ethics, trust, responsibility, and service may not be in a position to be competitive in an international culture that understands that these factors are the currency of success in business today. Once again, this text speaks to these issues and the authors are uniquely positioned to reflect on not only the importance of these concepts but also the steps that leaders can take to bring these concepts into practice right away in their organizations.

Finally, this title offers the reader some well positioned and current thoughts on leadership and change management. Once again, in an era of unprecedented inputs, complexity, and diversity, leadership has never been more important. While management will always be important, making the right leadership decision during complex times where multiple choices abound, is a point well illustrated in this text.

This book clearly informs the ever-evolving body of work in areas of leadership, change, and innovation. Their work here and the strategies they recommend are ready for implementation today and will no doubt serve to inform leaders for generations to come.

Casey Reason, Ph.D.
President of Highpoint Learning
www.caseyreason.com

Foreword

Conversations around Inclusion and Diversity are often awkward and ineffectual. The motives are numerous and recriminations abound. The research and stories shared within The Inclusive Leader: An Applied Approach to Diversity, Change, and Management is a refreshing and innovative blueprint for today's leader.

Diversity management, and more specifically inclusion is a key growth strategy in today's fiercely competitive global marketplace. In an increasingly global landscape, today's leader must have the political acuity and cultural competence to drive results and set the tone for how an organization treats its people authentically down to the roots of its business model. Companies that desire optimal positioning and relevancy will have to embrace diversity – in how they think, recruit, allocate, grow and innovate. Diversity is a reality that can no longer linger behind the "window dressing" model; rather it must become a part of the organizational brand that is created internally.

Dr. Rahim and Dr. Ayad have done a superb job in using empirical data and narrative to create a guide that offers concrete and actionable steps for leaders to follow and expand upon so they may leverage diversity as competitive advantage in the marketplace. The book helps leaders identify their ineffective practice and beliefs. If you are committed to an organizational belief system that harnesses the full potential its entire ecosystem, then, The Inclusive Leader: An Applied Approach to Diversity, Change, and Management is without question a required reading for current and future generation leadership.

Davine Bey, MBA
Director of Talent Acquisition, Cornell University
Co-founder, Global i365 LLC and CNY Inclusion Conference

Foreword

This book on diversity comes at an important time on our society. There is a current combative public discourse by prominent people with political and presidential aspirations about what kind of religions and what kind of immigrants are acceptable in America, which is a nation that was historically grown through the benefit of immigration. We are also engaged in a public civil rights dialog through lens of Black Lives Matter movement which is challenging the sense of duty, care, and intent of leaders that are paid by taxpayers to serve and protect. It is these historical events that make the knowledge in Ayad and Rahim's book so critical for supervisors at all levels.

The increased level of global immigration and national diversity has created huge need for those with uniquely specialized expertise in understanding the nuances of diversity and inclusion. Managing diversity is very complex when you consider challenge of making personal and professional interactions highly effective with employees with different senses of identity, culture, gender, races, ages, religions, languages, and ethnicities. The complexity is that organizations are putting professionals in leadership roles that have often have comprehension of the vast innovation that occurs in organizational cultures that are diverse, welcoming, and inclusive. The knowledge required to skillfully address the complex issues of valuing and celebrating diversity are not often the content of business related academic degree curriculum and courses. Consider if you are coaching a basketball starting 5 where only 3 players are playing offense and defense, while the others are just present? Your organization could be functioning the same way if the diverse voices and contributions of all employees are consistently present or considered.

Often organizational management narrowly views leadership competency in diversity narrowly as actions that protect the company from discrimination law suits or as job duties that oversee all of the annual required mandatory Equal Employment Training. Savvy managers realize that a true commitment to diversity is not about confusing activities with results or Band-Aid approaches or even annual cultural activities like Martin Luther King holiday celebrations and ethnic themed pot luck dinners.

Ayad and Rahim's book will give leaders the insight and wisdom that is required to be both knowledgeable in a time when this expertise is so vital and often absent in many organizations.

Dr. Darrell Norman Burrell
Certified Executive Coach and Diversity Consultant
Campus Director and Associate Professor, Florida Institute of Technology
Global Peace Maker Fellow, Claremont Lincoln University
2009 Presidential Management Fellow

Author's Foreword

This book is a revision and addition to our previous Amazon bestselling book "Leading Through Diversity: Transforming Manager into Effective Leaders". A revision because we have updated and expanded on the topics of leadership. An addition because we have added valuable material on diversity and inclusion. Our first book focused on presenting servant leadership as an effective leadership model while this book focuses on presenting an applied approach to diversity and inclusion as well as providing guidance to integrating diversity and inclusion into individuals and corporates' DNAs.

The study of leadership has roots in the beginning of civilization. The history of Egyptian rulers, Greek and Roman philosophers, and biblical stories shed light onto the various concepts of leadership. Interestingly, the debate around leadership remains fascinating and challenging. "Fascinating" because the concepts of leadership continue to evolve and generate lively debates. "Challenging" because the fundamental aspects of leadership confront an ever-changing world where the interaction of cultures and advancement of technology are redefining the world, let alone leadership. In addition, businesses, non-profit organizations, and governments are searching for what works to deliver on their promises, and on what makes sense to deliver on their ethical contract with customers and constituents. Oftentimes, what works may not make sense in the short run and / or may contradict the fundamental belief and culture of organizations and people. Consequently, leaders must anticipate evolving challenges, solve complex problems, and deliver results within a very short period of time after taking over a management or a leadership position.

Other aspects of this exciting and challenging debate have centered on the characteristics, traits, experiences, and skills that an effective leader or effective manager must possess, and whether effective leadership is born or taught. The terms to describe effective leadership include: Authentic Leadership, Servant Leadership, Thoughtful Leadership, Democratic Leadership, Authoritarian Leadership, Collective Leadership, Individual Leadership, Toxic Leadership, Situational Leadership, Transactional Leadership, Transformational Leadership, and Strategic Leadership. Similarly, different terminologies describe effective management styles: Process Management, People Management, Directive Democratic Management, Directive Autocratic Management, Permissive Democratic Management, Permissive Autocratic Management, Result-oriented Management, Micromanagement, and Macromanagement are just few of those terminologies.

Today, leaders and managers lead and manage a diverse workforce in a global economy. Language barriers, and religious, cultural and value differences pose new challenges that necessitate new leadership dynamics. Developments in technology, e-commerce, and virtual teams place a greater emphasis on workplace diversity and transforming the qualifications and skills that leaders and managers must possess.

In this book, we look into several underlying questions that other leadership and management scholars and practitioners have pondered over including:

- Can leaders and managers be one?
- Can the same person be an effective manager and an effective leader simultaneously?
- Can leadership and management responsibilities and roles overlap equally?
- Can we measure the effectiveness and efficiency in leadership and management?
- Can we teach leadership to non-experienced leaders?
- Can we define leadership by nature or nurture, or is it both?
- Is leadership and management a science, art, or both
- What is the role of diversity and inclusion in leadership and management?
- How can leaders achieve results by collaboratively serving their teams?

The following pages provide reflections, insights, and practical answers to all of the above stated questions.

This book also explores the challenges of management and leadership suggesting that transforming managers into effective leaders in a new era is possible and imperative for leading through diversity and innovations, and for creating an inclusive workplace. Most importantly, it offers a practical roadmap to achieving effective leadership.

Chapter 1

THE ART AND SCIENCE OF
LEADERSHIP AND MANAGEMENT

It has been stated that managers are people who do things right, and leaders are people who do the right thing. Other distinctions between leader and managers include: Transformational vs. Transactional, Leading People vs. Managing Tasks, Vision vs. Goals, Heart vs. Head, etc. While such distinctions serve to theoretically define disparate functional responsibilities, in reality roles of leadership and management blur since effective managers are also leaders and most leaders are often required to manage. Further, in reality it is impossible to imagine a functioning body that is solely transformational or transactional let alone imagining a function body with a head only or a heart only.

Personality, traits, analytical skills, communication styles, and people skills can often distinguish whether a person's natural inclination is best suited to lead and manage, manage, and / or lead. Nevertheless, it is widely accepted that leaders create a vision and inspire employees to translate the vision into reality while managers create and execute specific plans to translate the vision into tangible results. The smaller the business unit, the more managerial functions leaders assume but a business unit wouldn't have existed without visionary leadership nor it can survive without innovative leadership that anticipates, plans, and defeat the complexity, uncertainty, and unknowns of the future. Usually leaders display traits of innovation, grace, and inspiration while managers exhibit characteristics that tend to be functional, technical, administrative, command and control, and often expected to maintain or merely improve the status quo.

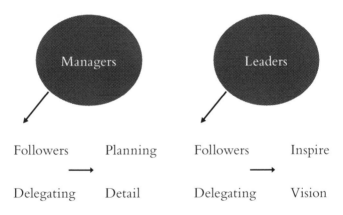

Followers   Planning   Followers   Inspire

Delegating   Detail   Delegating   Vision

Table # 1 further illustrates some differences between management and leadership:

Management Produces Order & Consistency	Leadership Produces Change & Movement
• Planning and Budgeting • Establishing Agendas • Setting Timetables • Allocating Resources	• Establishing Direction • Creating a Vision • Clarifying the Big Picture • Setting Strategies
• Organizing and Staffing • Provide Structure • Making Job Placements • Establishing Rules and Procedures	• Aligning People • Communicating Goals • Seeking Commitment • Building Teams and Coalitions
• Controlling and Problem Solving • Developing Incentives • Generating Creative Solutions • Taking Corrective Action	• Motivating and Inspiring • Inspiring and Energize • Empowering Subordinates • Satisfying Unmet Needs

Table # 1 – Source: Northouse, 2007, p. 10.

Caroselli, author of *Leadership Skills for Managers*, listed five duties that managers typically perform in the workplace:

1. They direct the flow of work within an organization versus performing it directly.
2. They perform human resource management-like duties that may involve the recruitment, hiring, development, termination, and disciplining staff.

3. They should exercise their authority role over-seeing the quality of work as well the staff's workplace environmental conditions.
4. They should assist in managing the communication channel between staff and upper management; acting as the staff liaison and resource linker.
5. They should motivate their staff to perform and contribute to the culture of the organization and its business practices by getting them to take ownership.

Just as Caroselli posited five traits of managers, he also identified five traits of leaders, emphasizing that leaders find it difficult being content with the status quo. He said leaders:

1. Want to always make a difference and inspire others.
2. Create something of value that did not exist before.
3. Generate positive energy in their environment.
4. Create and invite change; being a change agent.
5. Apply vision into action, developing tangible plans.

The Nature and Reality of Leadership & Management

Leadership is a combination of nature and nurture. A born leader may feel more comfortable in leadership roles than leaders who are learning leadership competencies by nurture. Interestingly, leaders who shaped the world such as Moses, Jesus, and Mohammed as well as Carl Marx, Pharos of Egypt, Emperors, and many other political, social, organizational, and religious leaders throughout history didn't attend formal leadership training courses even though they may have learned through "divine interventions" or family structures, experiences, and self-reflection.

When examining leadership traits and characters, there are several foundational questions to ask: What makes a leader a true leader? How do we measure leadership effectiveness? While leadership studies focus on the dynamic relationship between leadership concepts, leaders, and organizations, there are specific factors associated with leadership including technical, tactical, and analytical skills let alone character, charisma, knowledge, wisdom and judgment, creativity, communication, and courage.

Intrinsic capabilities (nature) and expertise (nurture) provide leaders the opportunity to develop approaches and strategies that are most appropriate for specific organizational environments and organizational goals. Regardless of how strong organizational culture is, people throughout the organization, especially large organizations, may perceive leadership differently. Consequently, in large organizations good leaders understand the role of culture and big ideas to unify and align people, actions, and organizational goals because the role of the leader is to actualize the purpose of the organization for the present and in the future. We support the idea that leadership is an action driven behavior, and "Leading-in-Action" necessitates a deep understanding of the leader's environment not only in the present but also in the future. This includes the culture, behavior, attitudes, history and thought-process of the leader's organization and its people. This renders leadership a collective responsibility with each member of the organization charged with delivering certain aspects of the organizational purpose. Conversely when employees disconnect from the purpose of the organization, accountability lie with the leaders because it is their responsibility to actualize the purpose of the organization in a sustainable manner. Consequently, one way to measure the effectiveness of leadership is through results as defined by the purpose of the organization.

Nevertheless, there are several inherited problems with strictly associating leadership with organizational goals and results. The environment may impact results in a subtle way. Functional knowledge, or a supportive management regime, may also impact results. In 1991, Buccino argued that the failures of 112,826 retailers in 1990, a 15% increase over 1989, were not the result of recession, but rather the result of internal problems. Specific management shortcomings identified as key contributors to business failure were:

1) Inadequate leadership - Effective management and supervision are key elements to achieving a competent and committed workforce. Usually, staff is an organization's most valuable asset, and it is important to help them become as productive as possible. Managers and supervisors have a pivotal role in positioning an organization as a facility of choice. However, most managers and supervisors cannot achieve this goal on their own.

2) Poor asset management – Most companies who do not have a clear idea of what proper assets assignments should be, have the potential to bring down the company. Sometimes companies invest in assets that only bring temporary advantage and then the asset is simply outgrown. With this thinking, the theory behind every advantage and idea proves that the company should assess and quantitatively evaluate potential investments.

3) Overexpansion – This management act would actually affect the whole organization financially. Most companies only see that expanding the

business guarantees more sales and let the business grow more. However, certain limitations accounted for as overexpansion can lead to bankruptcy if not carefully evaluated.

4) Inadequate controls – This refers to the ability of management to have control over different departments. Management should have control over all obligations, and should review, approve, and otherwise document all activities.

The ability to manage situations to the benefit of the organization is a critical leadership competency. Leaders should have creative ideas and see situations from a new perspective. As such, leaders should have the perseverance, the wisdom and the unwavering belief that situations are opportunities, not a fate to be accepted.

Styles of Leadership

Ancient forms of leadership focused on physical strengths. Leadership required fighting and winning on the battlefield. They earned their reputation by the amount of injuries they sustained and survived; let alone the number of battles they won. Eventually, thoughtful strengths evolved to intertwine with physical strengths. Perhaps King Richard and Saladin represented an image of this duality: courage and generosity. Eventually, farming communities and civil societies required different leadership styles, and the union between leadership, ideology, society, and economy became evident in reality as well as in research.

The industrial age impacted the way leaders perceived the world. The machine necessitated certain discipline in the behavior of leaders and followers; bureaucratic leadership thrived. Many leaders treated humans like machines and focused on efficiencies, quantification, predictability, and control. Time and motion studies to improve productivity boomed. Under such circumstances, individual workers became part of a machine that served productivity and efficiency of organizations. Most Leaders' perspectives adopted this reality and acted accordingly.

Such a view of leadership faced challenges because humans are not machines and it is impossible to operate based on such influences; thus leadership styles shifted to respond more favorably to human nature and evolving realities.

Servant leadership, ethical leadership, authentic leadership, transformational leadership, transactional leadership, charismatic leadership, collaborative leadership, autocratic leadership, democratic leadership, inspirational leadership, situational leadership, etc. are expressions that describe leaders' behaviors as they lead people and organizations. The adjectives describing the styles are self-explanatory; however, it is important to realize that leadership is about behaviors, and behaviors are usually the result of power, thought and beliefs. In most case, thoughts and beliefs are the result of experiences, environment, and culture. Since experiences, thoughts, culture, and situations vary greatly, it is safe to argue that there is no single style of effective leadership. Often leaders adapt their behavior to meet the needs of their followers and their particular environment.

From a behavioral perspective, leaders and managers may fall into four main classifications:

1. Directing (i.e. close supervision and specific instructions).

2. Coaching (i.e. close supervision, solicitation of ideas, and explanation of decisions).
3. Supporting (i.e. supportive and sharing of decision-making responsibilities).
4. Delegating (i.e. empower subordinates to own solving problems and decision making).

Executive presence is important to leadership style, but character is more important than "presence" because character defines "presence"; in fact personality and presence become a leadership burden without a strong moral character that acts with unwavering integrity.

Regardless of the behavioral style leaders adopt, their reaction to success and failure add to the overall perception of their effectiveness and style. Some leaders are totally intolerant to setbacks and they tend to take a deep analytical approach that is resistant to taking intuitive risks. Others encourage and reward intuitive risks and tend to have a high level of tolerance to failures that result in learning and the motivation to try again. Usually those leaders redefine success and failure and eventually end up encouraging workers to imagine beyond limits. They perceive failure as a long-term investment in the "learning organization" and success as a function of "daring" not a function of immediate results.

Practically, it seems futile to "box" leadership into a single dimension or expression. In fact, attempts to isolate leadership into one or few specific components are very dangerous because it may deprive leadership from its core purpose. From Enron to A.I.G. and from dictatorship to political and religious scandals there seems to be a clear distinction between the success and failure of leadership. Further, historic realities, theory, and practice agree on a set of critical competencies that inform, guide, and shape leadership.

Effective leadership must respond ethically and humanely to people whom are being led and to the mission that the group or organization is trying to accomplish. A person who is leading group of engineers to design a complex structure may use a different style than a person who is leading an army to defeat an enemy. Nevertheless, both leaders must be able manifest integrity, courage, humility, vision, sincerity, and exceptional communication skills to name a few competencies. Leaders use such competencies skillfully to create trust, inspiration, and energy to accomplish the task, goal, and / or mission. Typically, humans are motivated by "fear" of punishment, "hope" of rewards, combination of both "fear and hope", and / or higher purpose. Consequently, it is imperative for leaders to understand their team or followers and create the correct motivational dynamics. Effective leaders create a team that is motivated by a higher purpose because a sound purpose minimizes the ills and negativities that may come with rewards, punishments, and / or a combination of incentives and punishments.

For any purpose to become a living paradigm of an organization, effective leaders need a fertile imagination and exceptional two-way communication to create and / or define the purpose. This imagination, usually, evolves through time and is not the result of an overnight decision. While it is preferable for leaders to be visionary with big dreams, they often can surround themselves with talented people who possess imagination and can help the leader in creating the vision.

Two-way communication is critical for effective leaders to empower their followers to influence the purpose by their input and to allow the leader to communicate the vision for followers' buy-in and execution. One of the most important aspects of two-way communication is 360-feedback where effective leaders gather information to discover blind spots, strengths, and weaknesses of their personal behavior and vision through the eyes of the followers. 360-feedback becomes a futile exercise if it is not candid and sincere and / or if not followed by meaningful behavioral changes.

In the process of communication, effective leaders ask pertinent questions of key stakeholders within the organization, and use the data / feedback in a useful manner.

In 2002, Clutterbuck and Sheila provided a set of guidelines readily incorporated in every leader's toolbox of communication:

- Set mutual expectations clearly.
- Ensure that everyone has very clear objectives and performance measures.
- Plan and communicate the steps between where the team is now and where it needs to be.
- Give continuous feedback.
- Give people stretching goals but ensure they have all the support and resources they need to achieve the stretched goal.
- Recognize achievements.
- Encourage and establish team members' sense of self-belief.

In previously pages, we listed different styles of effective leadership and indicated that one way to measure the effectiveness of leadership is through results as defined by the purpose of the organization. We must assert that the extent to which a leader is able to flex her or his leadership style may define the effectiveness of leaders and their ultimate success. Leaders who are comfortable and / or limited to only one basic leadership style tend to be effective within specific situations. Other leaders who are able to modify their behavior to fit any situation tend to be more effective in multiple situations. We have witnessed situations where the entire organization changed reporting, language, and artifacts to align with a new leader where effectiveness would favor the other way around. Great leaders adapt to different situations.

Behaviors that build trust

Marriam-Webster dictionary defines trust as assured reliance on the character, ability, strength, or truth of someone or something. Managers, leaders, and academics agree that trust is critical to performance and success but it takes considerable amount of efforts and time to build, protect, and maintain trust. Further, trusting relationships remain fragile and subject to destruction in one instance of untrustworthiness. Below are twenty tested and verified behaviors that can build trust and performance:

1. Don't promise what you may not be able to deliver; let alone what you can't deliver
2. Be ready to take a "bullet", let alone hits, to protect your team
3. Demonstrate "care" by taking action at the expense of your personal time
4. Listen to all sides of the story before making a decision
5. Respect all perspectives especially those that disagree with your opinion

6. Appreciate the efforts of others especially when people fall short of goals
7. Reward mistakes that were intended to improve results and encourage calculated risks
8. Reward results, in a distinguished way, and hold people accountable
9. Eliminate favoritism as well as the perception of favoritism
10. Express happiness and positive emotions, avoid a poker face, and control your negative emotions
11. Be a student of your profession. Train your team
12. Be humble! Say I "don't know" when you don't know
13. Give all the credit to your team and take all the blame
14. Admit your mistakes and apologize for them… Sincerely
15. Don't avoid problems and don't cope with problems: Solve them
16. Be respectful, consistent, firm, and fair
17. Share information and encourage transparency
18. Do more than what you ask your team to do
19. Praise publicly and reprehend privately
20. Promote diversity and inclusion

Needless to say the list is not all-inclusive. Consequently building trust can be elusive, and it requires sincere efforts and investments.

The Interplay between Experience, Results, and Responsibility

Organizations, employees, and followers tend to view leaders in light of behaviors and results; success and setbacks assigned accordingly. Previous research has failed to demonstrate a consistent relationship between a leader's experience and results. With that in mind, in 2003, Derek, Scott, Kristin & Miguel looked at 29 head coaches in the National Basketball Association (NBA) during the 1996-97 seasons. The results indicated that leadership experience significantly predicted leader effectiveness after controlling for team members' abilities; results further suggested that highly relevant experience was a significantly better predictor than less relevant experience. Comparatively experience in the subordinate's job and experience under high-stress conditions significantly related to the leader effectiveness and supported incremental validity over traditional tenure measures of leadership.

The authors also found that with respect to organizational failures and successes, leadership roles attract more blame than other positions, but these roles do not attract more credit than lower-level roles. In addition, upper-level positions tend to assign greater blame than credit, while lower-level positions show a reverse pattern: they attract more credit than blame.

From a slightly different perspective, noted was a qualitative distinction between leadership responsibilities associated with the performance of day-to-day operations and involving face-to-face, or direct, leadership, in contrast to those leadership responsibilities linked to long-term preparation and planning/involving indirect leadership. The former would include, for example, enforcing individual/ group discipline, unit trainings, building unit cohesion whereas the latter would include strategic planning and change, structuring the organization, systemic performance measurement, adapting organizational culture, etc.

Leading a firm to success in today's market is difficult. An uncertain economy and unpredictable market changes make many employees uncertain of what to do. When leaders fail them, they either jump ship or stay on board floundering, and performing at reduced levels. In 2004 Sujansky asserted that "seven specific practices can set up even the best leaders to fall." These are:

1. Failure to trust.
2. Failure to shape and share a vision.
3. Failure to clearly define expectations.
4. Failure to model desired behaviors.
5. Failure to partner enough.
6. Failure to retain top talent.
7. Failure to celebrate success.

Who is really to blame? At what level does the leadership responsibility shift to another level, entity, or person?

Accountability, Responsibility, and Doing

It is important to distinguish between "accountability" and "responsibility" otherwise tasks may be jeopardized." Ultimately, leaders are accountable for the overall results of their organizations, and leaders assign individuals to be responsible for specific tasks, processes, business units, projects, etc. to deliver organizationally desired results. If every person in an organization is responsible for accomplishing a task, the task may never be accomplished. If the task is accomplished, it will likely be an inefficient outcome. Further, not assigning specific responsibilities create an environment of blame, and complacency. On the other hand, not creating an environment of teamwork leads to silos that deprive the organization from the ability to leverage resources.

Figure # 1 illustrates a relationship between "Managing" and "Leading" where the more time a person spends managing, the less time she / he has for leading and vice versa.

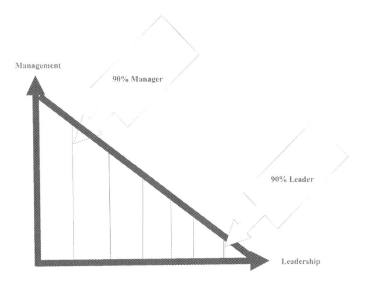

Figure #1

100% leading is a theoretical concept whereas 100% managing is not because employees can be hired to mere management without any leadership role (i.e. the graph implies that leaders who "manage" all the time miss the opportunity to lead and end up "chasing" the trend or problems). Figure #1 also implies that individuals are able to be managers and leaders simultaneously. Adjust figure #1 to construct the same relationship between doers / taskers on the Y axis and management / leadership on the X axis.

Leadership Development

Effective leaders find ways to creating businesses that shareholders adore, managers and employees trust and love, and customers vote for by their wealth and voices. Elliott Jaques calls it Global Organization Design; this design is an integrated system to implement leadership strategy that is internally consistent and delivers improved performance and profitability, aligns accountability, and creates clear roles and responsibilities.

In today's organizational environment, it is rare for a person to accidentally become a leader because organizations often set up formal and informal leadership developmental programs, 360 feedback surveys, annual performance reviews, and other initiatives to identify and promote leaders. Organizations realize that leadership is an evolving phenomenon where leaders learn, and develop new leadership competencies and skills in a dynamic and reciprocal way. There are three critical challenges that organizations face in developing leaders; they are:

1. Envisioning the "leader of the future".
2. Transforming today's leader into the "leader of the future" without negatively impacting today's results.
3. Maintaining a balance between ROI and retention.

The Leader of the Future

Restructuring the organization, what brought you here will not take you there, and first break all the rules are just few examples of expressions that are used to indicate a changing environment and rules in business and leadership.

Over the past decade, the co-authors' have held a fascination with organizations in desperate need to fill senior and corporate leadership roles. At times, it appeared organizational schisms existed between leaders who knew the "tricks of the trade" but didn't have what it took to transform the organization into the future, and outsiders, mostly MBA graduates with some experience, who didn't know the dynamics of the organization and its business needs. It appeared to be a battle between those who "know" but can't lead in the future and those who are polished to lead in the future but "didn't know" the specifics of the organization.

The Store Leadership Program at Home Depot was designed to bring leaders from outside the organization, teach them retail management, Home Depot style, and unleash their natural and nurtured skills to lead the organization into the next level. On paper, the program appeared outstanding. In reality, the program's challenge was organizational culture. The culture unequivocally rejected MBA graduates, coming from outside the organization, running around in Home Depot stores conducting Six Sigma projects and measuring employees' motions using a stopwatch.

A store manager at another reputable organization told us how his organization invested millions of dollars to introduce sophisticated wireless and computer capabilities into the organization but employees didn't even use the new technology because they were too busy tasking, and way underdeveloped for the technology. While Store Leadership Program clashed with existing culture, this initiative clashed with employees' skills, available resources, and operations.

Interestingly, and surprisingly, formal leadership internship programs are few and far between despite the fact that many aspects of leadership are developmental and easily taught. The majority of business leaders, today, develop through their experiences as practitioners and via formal education.

There are two critical components of leadership development:

1. Careful selection of assignments to enhance individual development as well as deliver business results i.e. learning-in-action.
2. Solid succession planning to assure a future pipeline of qualified leaders.

Hellriegel, Slocum, and Woodman make a compelling argument on the development of seven crucial fundamental capabilities or competencies critical to the development of leaders:

- **Managing Self-Competency**
  Involves the ability to assess your own strengths and weaknesses; set and pursue professional and personal goals; balance work and personal life; and engage in new learning, including new or changed skills, behaviors, and attitudes.

- **Managing Communication Competency**
  Involves the ability to transmit, receive, and understand information, ideas, thoughts, and feelings-nonverbally, verbally, in

electronic and written form, by listening, and other methods.

- **Managing Diversity Competency**
  Involves the ability to value unique individual and group characteristics, embrace such characteristics as potential sources of organizational strength, and respect the uniqueness of each individual.

- **Managing Ethics Competency**
  Involves the ability to incorporate values and principles that distinguish right from wrong in decision-making and behavior.

- **Managing Across Cultures Competency**
  Involves the ability to recognize and embraces similarities and differences among nations and cultures and then to approach key organizational and strategic issues with an open and curious mind.

- **Managing Team's Competency**
  Involves the ability to develop, support, facilitate and or lead groups to achieve organizational goals.

- **Managing Change Competency**
  Involves the ability to recognize and implement needed adaptations or entirely new transformations in the people, tasks, strategies, structures, or technologies in the person's area of responsibility.

Alternatively, Hooper and Potter proposed their own set of seven core leadership competencies:

- Setting direction.
- Emotional alignment.
- Acting as an example.
- Developing people at all levels.
- Effective communication.
- Acting as a proactive change agent.
- Effective behavior in crisis situations.

Table # 2 – Management and leadership: Yesterday vs. today and in the near future

Yesterday	Today
• Command and control	• Collaboration
• Long hours in the office	• Mobile
• Focus on input	• Focus on output
• Mechanical thinking	• Critical thinking
• Action oriented	• Results oriented
• Strong managerial skills	• Strong leadership skills
• Uniformity	• Diversity and inclusion
• Spontaneous	• Balance data and intuition

In *The Leadership Pipeline, How to Build the Leadership-Powered Company,* Charan, Drotter, and Noel discussed six passages a leader undertakes. The passages require more than a day or an academic course to master. This performance-based definition of potential turns the focus squarely on one's ability to do the job at their current leadership level. Performance becomes "the admission price" for growth and development. The strategy permits few, if any, shortcuts. This is because the leadership hierarchy is not a series of undifferentiated steps that would allow the energetic junior executive to skip a couple of stops on the way to the top. Instead, each management level involves a major change in job requirements, time, allocation, and work values—all requiring new learning and demonstrated mastery in leading.

Passage One: Managing Self to Managing Others

New, young employees usually spend their first few years with an organization as individual contributors. Whether they're in sales, accounting, engineering, or marketing, their skill requirements are primarily technical or professional. They contribute by doing the assigned work within given time frames and in ways that meet assigned professional standards. When people become skilled individual contributors who produce good results, especially when they demonstrate an ability to collaborate with others, they usually receive additional responsibilities. When they demonstrate an ability to handle these responsibilities and adhere to the company's values, they are often promoted to first-line manager.

Passage Two: Managing Others to Managing Managers

Managers must be "pure management". Before, individual contributions were still part of their job description. Now, they need to divest themselves of individual tasks.

This is also the point where managers must begin to think beyond their function and concern themselves with strategic issues that support the overall business. All this is difficult to do if a given manager at this passage still values individual contributions and functional work to the exclusion of everything else. They choose high technical achievers for first line managerial spots rather than true potential leaders; they are unable to differentiate between those who can do and those who can lead. Coaching is also essential at this level because first line managers frequently don't receive formal training in how to be a manager; they're dependent on their bosses to instruct them on the job.

Passage Three: Managing Managers to Functional Manager

Communication with the individual-contributor level now requires penetrating at least two layers of management, thus mandating development of new communication skills. What is just as significant, functional heads must manage some areas that are outside their own experiences. Team play with other functional managers and competition for resources based on business needs are two major transitional skills. This means participating in business team meetings and working with other functional managers. It is essential that functional managers delegate responsibility for overseeing many functional tasks to direct reports.

Passage Four: Functional Manager to Business Manager

Business managers usually receive significant autonomy, which people with leadership instincts find liberating. They also are able to see a clear link between their efforts and marketplace results. At the same time, this is a sharp turn; it requires a major shift in skills, time applications, and work values. The biggest shift is from looking at plans and proposals functionally (Can we do it technically, professionally, or physically?) to a profit perspective (Will we make any money if we do this?) and to a long-term view (Is the profitability result sustainable?).

New business managers must change the way they think in order to be successful. There are probably more new and unfamiliar responsibilities here than at other levels. Not only do they have to learn to manage different functions, but they also need to become skilled at working with a wider variety of people than ever before; the need to become more sensitive to functional diversity issues and communicating clearly and effectively. Even more difficult is the balancing act between future goals and present needs and making trade-offs between the two.

Passage Five: Business Manager to Group Manager

A business manager values the success of his own business. A group manager values the success of other people's businesses. This is a critical distinction because some people only derive satisfaction when they're the ones receiving the lion's share of the credit. The leadership pipeline clogs with business managers who aren't operating at peak capacity due to lack of support or their authority usurped.

This level also requires a critical shift in four skill sets. First, group managers must become proficient at evaluating strategy for capital allocation and deployment purposes. This is a sophisticated business skill that involves learning to ask the right questions, analyze the right data, and apply the right corporate perspective to understand which strategy has the greatest probability of success and therefore should be funded.

Coaching new business managers is also an important role for this level. The third skill set has to do with portfolio strategy. This is quite different from business strategy and demands a perceptual shift. Considerations are which businesses to: add, subtract, or change position us properly and assure current and future earnings?

Fourth, group managers must become astute about assessing whether they have the right core capabilities to win. Leadership becomes more holistic at this level. People may master the required skills but they won't perform at full leadership capacity if they don't begin to see themselves as a broad-gauged executive. By broad-gauged, we mean that managers need to factor in the complexities of running multiple businesses, thinking in terms of community, industry, government, and ceremonial activities. They need to evolve their perspective to the point that they see issues in the broadest possible terms.

Passage Six: Group Manager to Enterprise Leader

When the leadership pipeline clogs at the top, it harms all leadership levels. The transition to the sixth passage focuses on values than skills. As leaders of an institution, they must be long term, visionary thinkers. At the same time, they must develop the operation mechanisms to know and drive quarter by-quarter performance that is in tune with longer-term strategy. The tradeoffs involved can be mind-bending as enterprise leaders learn to value these trade-offs. In addition, this new leadership role often requires well-developed external sensitivity an ability to manage external constituencies, sense significant external shifts, and do something about them proactively (rather than reactively).

Enterprise leaders must let go of the pieces (the individual products and customers) and focus on the whole (e.g., how well do we conceive, develop, produce, and market all products to all customers). Finally, at this level a CEO must assemble a team of high-achieving and ambitious direct reports, knowing that some of them want his job and picking them for the team despite this knowledge. The preparation for the chief executive position is the result of a series of diverse experiences over a long time. The best developmental approach provides carefully selected job assignments that stretch people over time and allow them to learn and practice necessary skills

Perhaps the shortest and safest way to position current leaders for the future is to encourage and support them in self-development journey towards the future. The role of the organization is to provide resources and the role of leaders is to provide commitment and contribution. Needless to say, the details of this relationship depend on numerous factors within different organizations, but the relationship should be contractual within employment benefits and responsibilities.

In 2005, Ferrarie confirmed that Shell put efforts on developing the skills that a leader needs as something that begins at the recruiting stage and continues throughout the length of an employee's time with the company. With tools to assess leadership potential, based on a framework of desired leadership competencies, employees are better able to understand and achieve their full potential, while the company can better judge the shape and needs of its talent pool for senior leaders. Shell nurtures leadership from the beginning to the end.

Big companies are beginning to think small by identifying their best risk-takers, placing them in charge of highly motivated internal entrepreneurial, intrapreneurial venture teams, and developing new products as expediently as possible. According to Kuzela, 1984, Du Pont Co. (Wilmington, Delaware) began such teams 30 years ago and developed successful new ideas and items. There is an element of risk attached to leaders applying learned experiences proactively. Often this risk will create new directions, innovations, or initiatives.

There is a long and wide stream of character qualities embedded in leadership, but leadership is much more. Integrity is a vital and lethal component of leadership. Ethical leaders must engage in acts or behaviors that benefit others, and must refrain from acts or behaviors that harm others. For example, a leader charged to solve a problem should have the courage to overcome fears and criticisms from other people. He or she should know how to face challenges and guide employees to achieve a vision that would lead the organization to growth. The will to sacrifice, the passion to fulfill the dreams of other people, and the motivation to inspire others to grow and add value to the world are important competencies of leaders. In solving the problem ethical leaders (i.e. effective leaders) provide followers with a voice because ethical leaders share power and naturally empower followers. In contrast, Howell and Avolio, 1992, described unethical leadership as self-absorbing and manipulative i.e. leaders who manipulate power to serve their self-interests, who are insensitive to follower's needs and have little regard for behaving in socially constructive ways.

One aspect of the art of leadership is intuition. Leaders often recount the gut feeling that drives them to success.

Many executives and managers embrace intuition as an effective approach to important decisions. Indeed, recent surveys and business press articles indicate broad support for the use of intuition when making strategic decisions. The need for quick decisions, the need to cope with demands created by complex market forces, and the assumed benefits of applying deeply held knowledge combine to create strong perceived value for the intuitive approach. Intuition, however, remains an unexplored phenomena, not yet subjected to sufficient review, particularly in a forum for executives and other managers.

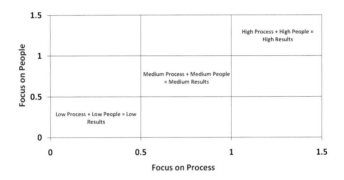

Figure # 2

Figure # 3

Figure # 2 illustrates a relationship between a focus on process vs. a focus on people and figure # 3 illustrates a relationship between a focus on results and a focus on leadership's behaviors. While both graphs assume a linear relationship and a positive correlation, in reality some amazing leaders deliver low results, and some very disruptive behaviors deliver high results. Similarly a focus on people can lead to a chaotic process, and a focus on processes can be at the expense of people. In the two figures, however, we argue that great managers and great leaders maximize the output of processes and results in a sustainable way by a focus on people and behaviors.

Figure #4

Figure #4 illustrates how entry level work can lead to higher responsibilities. In the "real-world" sometime you should place a person in a position to stretch the person and sometimes you should place a person in a position to stretch the position. Great team-members stretch their positions and raise their hands for additional responsibilities.

Conclusions

Leadership is a combination of nature and nurture and leaders are born and created. While it is possible to define key elements that are associated with management and elements that are associated with leadership, in reality, the roles of management and leadership blur depending on situations, organizations, and the tendencies of people. Leaders are accountable for the overall results of their organizations as well as for the wellbeing for organizations and civic duty towards society and the world. Perhaps one of the best ways to create effective organizations is to design the work where supervisors manage tasks and people, managers manage processes and people, and leaders manage managers and businesses. It is a question of time allocation: The more a person tasks the less this person supervises. The more a person supervises the less this person plans. The more a person plans the more this person manages and the less he or she supervises. The more one manages and reflects the more this person envisions, motivates, inspires, and leads.

Organizations design programs to attract, develop, and retain leaders for the present and the future. The active practice of leadership is a developmental process, a learned-reflective-nature. The key to learned leadership is to apply the wisdom of learned knowledge to the ever-changing environment. Therein lies the measure of leadership, the ability to discern and adapt to each moment as a unique occasion. Adding what one knows and application is fundamental to leadership development and measurement. Each experience provides a unique Developmental–Learning opportunity. Leaders can use those "applied context" occasions as training opportunities for emergent leaders.

It is not possible to isolate leadership and actions from the social and political pressures that surround the situation. Innovation and the creation of new ways to overcome obstacles become critical for successful leadership. Integrity and standing up for what's right is vital for effective leadership.

Chapter 2

DIVERSITY AND INCLUSION AS A LEADERSHIP ASSET

The Dynamics of Diversity in USA

The concept of diversity is evolving with a rapidly changing world. In the earlier days of the United States, the country was geographically isolated on the North American continent bordered by oceans, Canada, and Mexico. The country developed its place in the world through internal growth and cultural socialization based on American norms, values, and traditions. Most of US citizens grew up only knowing one language, English. Only a tiny percentage of the population had ever been out of the country. Even in the 1940s, at state level, let alone organizational levels, the United States foreign diplomats often did not speak the language of their assigned countries, knew little of the culture, and as a consequence were limited in their ability to engage and understand other societies.

To further understand the dynamics of diversity, take into consideration the following effects:

1. Increased cultural and ethnic immigration to the US from groups with background of different languages and diverse religions.
2. The growth of international business, global competition, and international outsourcing.
3. The increased presence and impact from international telecommunications including e-mail and internet technologies.
4. Changes in work-values and perception of the world between "baby boomers" and their children.
5. Individuals began increasingly to celebrate their differences and not open to compromising their racial, religious, cultural, and other apparent differences.

According to Friedman, 2007, the fall of the Berlin Wall helped flatten the alternatives to international capitalism and unlock enormous pent-up energies for hundreds of millions of different cultural, racial, and religious backgrounds in places like India, Brazil, China, and the former Soviet Empire. It also allowed Americans to look at the world differently and to see it more as a seamless whole. Because the Berlin Wall was not only in our way; it was blocking our sight and our ability to think about the whole world as a single market, a single ecosystem, and a single community.

For many businesses, organizations, and business leaders, diversity was a compliance issue managed by Human Resources professionals with some legal and moral implications. Today, diversity has evolved to becoming a business imperative that incorporates a wide range of elements including traditional aspects such as race, gender, etc. to elements such as sexual orientation, leadership styles, personal preferences, education, language, and diversity of talent and contribution.

The Business Case for Diversity

Aside from legal and moral implications, there are obvious benefits to a diverse workforce including:

1. Diverse workforce attracts diverse customer base; consequently improved market share
2. Diverse workforce provides organizations with flexibility to expand internationally i.e. provides insights into cultural differences, improved networking opportunities, etc.
3. Diverse workforce attracts talent from different backgrounds resulting in stronger organizations
4. Embracing and accepting differences at work contribute to reduction in turnover and improving productivity
5. Accepting and embracing differences at work creates a culture that is adaptable and flexible to change and potential change management interventions

Imperial research, including research conducted by the National Urban League, supports the conceptual business case provided in above stated 5 main points.

Melting Pot or Colorful Salad

Melting pot, or we are all the same, sounded like a noble goal that offered and promoted equality and equal opportunities. The concept of a melting pot has a positive connotation when different cultures and backgrounds come together to create a unified texture where all ingredients lose their original uniqueness to create a new taste. The salad metaphor, on the other hand, proposes a new taste by keeping the uniqueness of the original ingredients.

The purpose of this paragraph is not to favor one model over the other or one metaphor on the other because that may contradict "diversity" concepts and tend to be philosophical while the main purpose of this book is "practice and application". On the contrary, while both metaphors serve as examples on how diverse and complex realities are, both metaphors provide guidance for business leaders into different models of diversity.

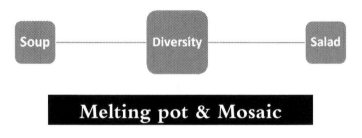

Figure #1 – Integration vs. Assimilation Models

From a business perspective, the main objective of diversity and inclusion is to utilize available talent and resources internally and externally and benefit from differences and similarities to optimize business results.

Three vital steps can achieve this:

1. At the board level, align diversity with business model and resources. At the "employee and management" levels, link diversity and inclusion

to performance management and performance rewards.

2. Communicate the critical role of diversity and inclusion to all employees, shareholders, business partners, and customers.

3. Create training programs tailored to the specific culture and need of the organization.

Diversity and Inclusion: Global vs. International

An organization, or a leader, may adopt diversity and inclusion within a business unit, country, multiple countries, and even internationally without being truly and fully "diverse and inclusive". A fully diverse and inclusive organization, or leader, is one that embraces the universe i.e. global and universal in nature.

For example, an organization that conducts business in two or more countries may be classified as international or multinational but not necessary global. A global company conducts business in most countries of the world but most importantly its culture and DNA incorporates the global dynamics. For example, those companies strive for reducing and / or managing global warming, global treaties, and global norms in a way that is not threatening to any culture; on the contrary, a global company perceives the culture of the world as part of the DNA of the organization. This doesn't create contradictions within global companies, i.e. differences between cultures; on the contrary, it creates harmony. For example, globally inclusive companies are able to accommodate contradictory norm by proper work design, cultural awareness, and respect for all people. In such an environment a Muslim female who doesn't shake hands (with "non-close family members") feels welcome and understood at a USA branch company and similarly a Christian woman feels welcome and understood when eating pork at a Jordan branch location.

Let us discuss marketing as an example. According to the Oxford University Press, global marketing means a company adopts the same promotional tactics across the world – think of Wal-Mart or Nike. In global marketing, the business thinks of the whole world as its operating space and does not adapt its products or services, communication and distribution channels to domestic requirements.

International marketing, on the other hand, means the strategy a company applies when it opens a subsidiary in a country and lets the affiliate serve the local market, paying attention to local customs in terms of religion, lifestyles and eating habits, for example:

1. In global marketing, a company offers the same products and services across the board, i.e. multiple countries. Think about banks, insurance companies and large retail chains like Wal-Mart. In international marketing, products and services are countries specific. Think about Sharia finance products, offered only in Islamic countries or to Muslim customers in non-Muslim countries – or meat banned from kosher or halal diet.

2. Global marketing personnel tend to work at the company's headquarters and generally are a diverse group of people. They possess various skills that collectively mesh well together, and take a global view of the company's market. Conversely, in international marketing, team members tend to hail exclusively from the same country or a country

with linguistic or cultural affinity with the primary country.

3. The global marketing team manages the budget directly from the corporate headquarters. For example, Nike sets a global marketing budget which then trickles down to local offices. In international marketing, however, the subsidiary negotiates and handles budget issues at the local level. Take for example McDonalds, which runs local ads, some of which you will never see in another country.

4. When it comes to promotion tactics, global marketing teams try to run ads and other communication ploys that are in sync with a global audience. An excellent way to understand this? Look at the 2014 FIFA World Cup ads – a perfect mix for global marketing: global sports event, billions of viewers, one passion for the game. International marketing, on the other hand, tailors commercials and other promotion tactics for the local market.

5. Marketing does not mean you sit in a corner office and think about how to sell a product. The typical marketing mix has four components, what experts call the 4Ps: product, price, promotion and place (of distribution). So in terms of operational autonomy, global marketing teams tend to run everything from A to Z, from the corporate headquarters, whereas international marketing teams handle things domestically.

6. By reviewing their social media pages, you can quickly see which companies favor global marketing over international marketing – and vice versa. For example, you will notice that McDonald's adopts an international marketing strategy, with Facebook

pages as diverse as McDonald's Malaysia, McDonald's Brazil, McDonald's Italia and McDonald's Polska (Poland). Conversely, Nike or Caterpillar runs a single page.

7. Customer engagement is more active in international marketing. By setting multiple communication channels, a company can better engage with fans and customers at a local level. That is not to say that global marketing is less effective when it comes to customer engagement – the tactics are just different. But it is clear that international marketing tends to produce a higher level of engagement than global marketing.

8. In global marketing, commercials run all over the world, whereas international marketing favors ad airing in the local market exclusively – or in similar markets, at most. Some products lend themselves pretty well to global advertising. We already talked about sport gear; you also have movies and songs as well as technology products. Other products, conversely, cannot exist in some countries because of cultural prohibition or legal censorship.

9. Market research and R&D are as deep and broad in global marketing as they are in international marketing. Sometimes, though, global marketing can produce big flops when market research has not properly conducted or local customs thoroughly studied. Think, for example, of Chevy Nova's and Mazda LaPuta's unfortunate stints in the Spanish market. (In Spanish, 'no va' and 'la puta' mean 'it doesn't go' and 'the whore,' respectively). Other product flops include the Ben-Gay aspirin,

McDonald's Arch Deluxe, and the Cocaine Energy Drink produced by Redux Beverages.

10. Our number 10 example is not really an example of comparative global marketing vs. international marketing analysis, but an illustration of how a hybrid structure, international and global, can help companies succeed. Coca-Cola's use of that mixed tactic was effective in the earlier days, and was subsequently adopted and followed by every company, from Mercedes Benz to Frito Lay to Procter & Gamble to McDonald's.

Whether a company opts for international marketing or global marketing is, after all, company management's decision. Ultimately, the selected marketing strategy must fit the organization's vision, mission, brand policy and operational structure. Needless to say, a company must reach a comfortable operational size before adopting a global marketing strategy.

Diversity and Inclusion, Cyborgs, and the Workplace

A cyborg is a being with both organic and biomechatronic parts. Biomechatronics is an applied interdisciplinary science that aims to integrate mechanical elements, electronics and parts of biological organisms. Merriam-Webster dictionary defines a cyborg as "a person whose body contains mechanical or electrical devices and whose abilities are greater than the abilities of normal humans". Oxford dictionary adds specificity to the definition by stating that a cyborg is "a fictional or hypothetical person whose physical abilities are extended beyond normal human limitations by mechanical elements built into the body".

Interestingly, the scope of these different definitions ranges from mere mechanical and / or electrical integration into the biological organisms, including humans, all the way into totally transforming humans beyond human capacity.

Accordingly, a cyborg is a being assisted by different elements, and the following typology is proposed:

> A. Pure Cyborg: A cyborg whose life and functions depend on the electrical, mechanical, biological, and / or other parts without the original human soul.
>
> B. Permanent Cyborg: A human being whose life and / or functions depend on the electrical, mechanical, biological, and / or other implanted elements
>
> C. Temporary Cyborg: A human being whose life depends on the continuity of original human soul and whose functions are assisted by electrical, mechanical, biological, and / or other elements.

A robot can be classified as a being without biological organs, but the future belongs to cyborgs not robots as 3D bioprinting, tissue engineering, and artificial intelligence sciences mature.

Intentionally, this proposed typology doesn't list "pure human" as an independent type because it is hard to imagine a human who is not, also, a temporary cyborg. In fact, from the early days of our history we utilized elements to help us enhance our performance. For example, we used canes to support our bodies, gloves to protect hour hands, eyeglasses to enhance our visions, and microscopes to see what's invisible to our eyes. A human in a car is a temporary cyborg (i.e. implanting the human in a device vs. implanting the device in a human). A human with an artificial arm, artificial kidney, and / or artificial heart pump is a permanent cyborg if this human was born with a human soul, but a pure cyborg if was built without the original human soul.

Beyond the scope of this book there are two critical topics that we plan to tackle in the future:

1. The philosophical discussion around our ability to create a human soul from scratch
2. The advantages and disadvantages of this particular typology

While future research and regulations may set the boundaries to the specific amount of biomechatronic elements to be added and / or implanted that justify taking a being from a pure human to a temporary cyborg, we may need to get used to working and interacting with robots including the self-driven cars and cyborgs with different types of permanent and temporary implants and / or performance enhancement devices.

With the inevitable entry of cyborgs to the workplace, the debate around the consequences of automation and artificial intelligence continues. Some argue that the next generation of robots will prove disastrous to humans while others assert that the next generation of robots will contribute to the end of scarcity and the beginning of the euphoric age of abundance.

There is a big difference between the tools of productivity and the plight of economy. Eventually, the tractor or any form of productivity improvement didn't contribute to the decline of communism, to the end of empires throughout history, or to the current triumph of capitalism. It is ideas, policies, rules, regulations, leadership, sacrifices, and energy and ambitions of humans that dictate major changes of humans and their realities.

There is no doubt that the cyborgs and their primitive predecessors (i.e. robots) will improve productivity and will change our world in the same way that air travel (i.e. machine) has made the world smaller. Yet it is the regulations and human-made rules that forced Syrian refugees to pay over $1000 traveling via boats with significant risks, including death, instead of paying $500 traveling via a safer mode (i.e. airlines).

Tackling the implication of human intelligence (i.e. innovation) in isolation of human ideologies or regulation and politics is very deceptive. Consequently, we propose that the future of workplace and society will be shaped by ideas and regulations not by cyborgs; even if cyborgs dominated humans. Diversity and inclusion will continue to be a vital driver of organizational effectiveness, and the faster organizations adjust to accommodate cyborgs, the more effective such organizations will be; both on the short term and on the long term. Companies that are struggling today to accommodating humans from different backgrounds will face serious weaknesses as cyborgs, let alone new generations with new view of the world, start entering the workplace. If we advocate diversity and inclusion today, we will have a better chance coexisting with each other and with cyborgs. In fact, we will have brighter future for the following reasons:

1. We will be more productive and more efficient
2. We will be more intelligent in the way we solve problems for all (i.e. thoughtfully, kindly, etc.)

3. We will be more appreciative of what machines can't do
4. We will be able to dispel the myth that machines are harmful to humans
5. Arguably, we will be more humane due to the uniqueness of the "human soul", inability to create human soul from nothingness, and the ultimate dominance of "human cyborgs"

Needless to say, we can't fully dismiss the bleak picture of a future where cyborgs and humans interact based on the worst characteristics of humans and machines (i.e. injustice and discrimination or malfunctions and glitches).

Developing the Diverse Leader

Transforming managers into effective leaders necessitates growing the inclusive leader inside managers. We propose a deep reflection process and participatory training as means to develop inclusive leaders.

Case Study

Dr. Emad Rahim interviewed three organizational leaders of diverse ethnic, cultural, and religious backgrounds to assess the issue of religious and cultural diversity in organizations, and to make recommendations on how to improve content and delivery of diversity training. The interviewees were organizational leaders with over 10 years of management experience and each one had an advanced degree. The participants were from a variety of diverse backgrounds and countries including Afghanistan, female (Islam), African American, male, (Christianity), and Jewish

American, female (Judaism). All of the participants were bilingual.

These leaders had recently completed diversity training and queried, individually, about the value and need for diversity training to include, beyond race and color, an international, cultural and diverse religious component. The involvement of a diverse group of participants in the problem assessment, data collection, and solution development created an opportunity to benefit from a wide variety of perspectives, innovations, and ideas. A broader set of backgrounds and attitudes to problem solving can permit the propensity of more creative solutions to develop

The interviewees' feedback discussions followed the eight steps outlined in 2008 by Cummings and Worley noted below:

1. Outlining the nature of the problem.
2. Using the researcher as the facilitator and organizer of the intervention.
3. Amassing facts and information about the problem.
4. Soliciting opinion and perspectives.
5. Developing a collective analysis of the problem.
6. Developing a joint plan of attack for the problem.
7. Developing an action intervention.
8. Evaluating the results of the intervention.

After the individual interview results, the three organizational leaders formed a discussion focus group. The goal of this collaboration provided an opportunity for them to share, discuss, and develop a consensus and make recommendations to improve diversity training based on the perspectives developed from their individual interviews. The group was shown the slides used in the on-line training and were asked to debate, critique, and discuss the training. They also identified the concepts of the training that were the strongest and subsequently invited to suggest improvements. As discussed by Thatchenkery and Metzker, 2006, the focus was on seeing the best in the current diversity program and developing an innovative framework to improve the program focusing on aspect of building strengths. With each discussion topic, the group was required to brainstorm and come up with answers based on their experiences at the agency and knowledge of cultural diversity.

The individual interviews discussions yielded the following themes consistently.

1. The benefits of a sound diversity training program outweigh any possible organizational liabilities, internal or external.
2. The benefits of a program that includes religious and cultural diversity include educating employees on racial, cultural, and religious differences of employees so that employees more sensitive, compassionate, and culturally competent.
3. The benefits of a program that includes improved employee morale. When employees feel respected and valued they are more likely to feel more committed to the organization. Demoralized, resentful workers are not conducive to a healthy and nurturing work environment.
4. Management training. All managers should be required to have goals or activities related to developing competencies geared towards providing a work culture that values diversity. This could also include additional training for managers in terms

of recruiting, hiring, retention and promotions as it relates to diversity issues.

As Tomas, 1991, asserted it is difficult for managers who work with diverse employees to comprehend all the issues. Thus, leaders must move from "unconscious incompetence", where they don't know when and how they offended others, to "conscious competence" where they know and act on how to respect and include others.

Organizations often assume that through training courses the organization can dictate and / or change how workers feel, think, and act with regards to diversity. Training alone does not produce sustainable behavioral adjustments let alone behavioral changes. Creating a culture where employees are sensitive, culturally competent, respectful, and inclusive requires commitment, resources, and consequences i.e. rewards from senior leadership. The commitment starts with unwavering and sincere realization that one is not superior or inferior to anyone else based on race, sex, ethnicity, ability, place of origin, wealth, inherent culture, etc. This sincere realization allows organizations to create relationships based upon meaningful and productive traits such as commitment, dedication, honesty, trust, and mutual respect to name a few. This will not only naturally, lead to ethical leadership but also effective organizations.

The benefit of the previously described was that employees were active participants in the evaluation of their work climate and training. Employees used their organizational knowledge and expertise to develop a sound strategy for taking the best aspects of the diversity training and viable recommendations on how to improve the process and make it more comprehensive as it relates to cultural, racial, ethnic, and religious diversity.

Whether it was Sears, Home Depot, Walmart, or privately owned companies, the first author has witnessed not only the positive impact of diversity on business results but also effective ways to create the diverse team and diverse culture. In one situation, in a team building exercise, the first author divided his team into three different groups with the purpose of building the best "bird house". The first team was comprised of employees where the majority belonged to the "operations" side of the organization, the majority of the second team was comprised of employees from the "merchandising" side of the organization, and the third team was a diverse team from all sides of the organization including human resources. Interestingly, the first team built a very solid birdhouse that made landing, entering, and exiting easy for the birds, but the birdhouse was heavy, complex, and unattractive; clearly they focused on the functionality of the structure (i.e. operations). The second team built a birdhouse that was beautiful in its design but very unstable as a structure. However, the diverse team built a birdhouse that was beautiful and stable at the same time. When a group of people work together with different perspectives, the team will bring to the table the strengths of these differences but also may create challenges. For example, while watching the dynamics of the three teams while in action, the first author noticed that both the operations inclined team and merchandising inclined team were acting without too many arguments or discussions. They had a clear operating reference i.e. the work was almost mechanic. On the other hand, the diverse team got into couple of serious discussions on strategy and operating principles. After the exercise the three groups engaged in discussions about the concepts of diversity and realized its importance. While diversity was not the main purpose of the exercise, it became part of it due to the awareness of the leader. It is that deliberate realization of diversity as well as the presence of the concept as a state of mind coupled by the encouragement of the organization that integrated diversity into the exercise not an official training curriculum. Needless to say, formal training is critical but it isn't sufficient by itself.

In another situation, the first author invited his team (7 leaders who manage over $80 million business with over 300 employees each) to take a questionnaire that determines their natural behavioral inclinations. The team then engaged in discussions about their preferences. As a leader, the first author was able to build on each member's strengths to create an organization that leverages diverse talent and to strengthen the dynamics of the team by understanding each member to the other and how uniquely each member contributes to the success of the team and how the team collectively contributes to the success of each member.

Some cultural difference that diverse leaders need to be aware of

Table # 1 – Cultural awareness

Action	Culture A	Culture B
Looking someone in the eyes	Nothing to hide /straight talker	Sign of disrespect / Challenge
Saying someone is old	Offensive statement	Statement of respect / With age comes wisdom
Shaking hands or hugs between different genders	A way to greet and show kindness	A sign of disrespect / Offensive religiously
Holding hands and kissing on the cheek for same gender	A declaration of homosexuality	Greeting / Close friendship
Saying: Come on and hit me / let us get done with it	Inciting violence	Declaring surrender / Inciting calm
Money	High value / sign of success	Just a means / Deeds what counts
Time	Time is money	Important but not top value
Family	Pictures can be shared with others	Very private
Pets	Part of family	Keep away

The list indicated in table # 1 is by no means inclusive, only meant to give an idea about how simple things can be offensive to some. To get a detailed understanding of cultural differences, try to engage people especially those who you work and / or interact with. Observe and learn but equally important ask questions to learn about others.

Topic	Non-Inclusive Leader	Inclusive Leader
Meetings	Agenda dictated and / or heavily influenced by the leader	Input from all participants
Meetings	Leader presents the most and / or comments the most on every presentation	Group discussions
Meetings	Participants are not encouraged to speak	Participants are encouraged to speak up
Conflicts	Avoidance	Resolution
Conflicts	Political approach	Resolution
Goals	Individual	Group / team
Execution	Metric driven	Results are achieved based on diverse thoughtfulness and integrity

Tactics	Mix fear with hope i.e. promotions and / or performance improvement plans	Use up-to-date methods, processes and tools including performance development plans
Approach	Limited new ideas	Invites new ideas
Scope	Local, regional, and perhaps international	Global, and perhaps universal
Approach	Authoritative	Inspirational

Table #2 – Behaviors of inclusive leaders

Similar to table #1, table # 2 is not inclusive but it presents contrasts between inclusive and non-inclusive leaders and most importantly expected behaviors of inclusive leaders.

The Journey of diversity and inclusion

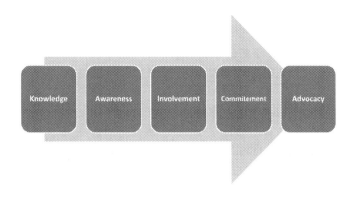

Figure # 2 – The journey of diversity and inclusion

Figure #2 illustrates the journey of diversity and inclusion. It starts with information and knowledge. A key element of this information is the fundamental right of human beings to live free with responsibility for actions. Other elements of knowledge include the fundamental right of equality in legal and civic terms as well as the appreciation of openness and differences. Perhaps the most important aspect of awareness is self-awareness around biases and cultural sensitivity. Moving from intellectual curiosity and knowledge to action is a vital step achieved through involvement in diversity and inclusion activities. This involvement will produce change; change is never easy especially when coupled with behavioral and emotional newness. Consequently, commitment is another key requirement for this journey. It means perseverance and ability to overcome adversity. It means ability to see obstacles as opportunities and to believe that the capacity of solutions exceeds the complexity of problems. Advocacy is the peak of this journey where a person becomes openly active in supporting diversity and including as well as in behaving as an inclusive and diverse human being.

University of Arkansas Medical Science Cultural Sensitivity Test

We find University of Arkansas Medical Science Cultural Sensitive test a great tool to better assess one's self on cultural sensitivity. Cultural sensitivity is something we all like to think we have. Clearly tied to empathy, the capacity to put ourselves into another person's shoes and see the world from his/her viewpoint. Cultural sensitivity is an essential quality for peaceful and harmonious living in a society that admits, within the law, many different ways of thinking and behaving. Low cultural sensitivity is associated with authoritarian personalities and also with narrow and limited experience of the world. While it is easy to detect low cultural sensitivity in others, it is not so easy to pin it down in ourselves. This questionnaire, however, if answered honestly and accurately, will give you some pointers. Tabulate your own score:

1. When a friend does something you very much disapprove of, do you
    a. Break off the friendship
    b. Tell him how you feel, but keep in touch
    c. Tell yourself it is none of your business, and behave toward him as you always did.

2. Is it hard for you to forgive someone who has seriously hurt you?
    a. Yes
    b. No

    c.   It is not hard to forgive him, but you don't forget.

3.   Do you think that
    a.   Censorship is vitally necessary to preserve moral standards?
    b.   A small degree of censorship may be necessary (to protect children, for instance)?
    c.   All censorship is wrong?

4.   Are most of your friends people
    a.   Very much like you?
    b.   Very different from you and from each other?
    c.   Like you in some important respects, but different in others?

5.   You are trying to work and concentrate, but the noise of children playing outside distracts you. Would you
    a.   Feel glad that they are having a good time
    b.   Feel furious with them
    c.   Feel annoyed, but acknowledge to yourself that kids do make noise

6.   If you were traveling abroad and found that conditions were much less hygienic than you are used to, would you
    a.   Adapt quite easily
    b.   Laugh at your own discomfort
    c.   Think what a filthy country it is

7. Which virtue do you think is most important?
   a. Kindness
   b. Honesty
   c. Obedience

8. Do you discuss critically one friend with others?
   a. Often
   b. Rarely
   c. Sometimes

9. If someone you dislike has a piece of good luck, would you
   a. Feel angry and envious
   b. Wish it had been you, but not really mind
   c. Think Good for him

10. When you have a strong belief, do you
    a. Try very hard to make others see things the same way as you
    b. Put forward your point of view, but stop short of argument or persuasion
    c. Keep it to yourself unless directly asked.

11. A friend is suffering from depression. Everything in his life seems to be fine, but he complains to you that he always feels depressed. Would you
    a. Listen sympathetically
    b. Tell him to pull himself together
    c. Take him out to cheer him up

12. Would you employ someone who has had a severe nervous breakdown?
    a. No
    b. Yes, provided there was medical evidence of complete recovery
    c. Yes, if he was suitable in other ways for the work

13. When you meet someone who disagrees with your views, do you
    a. Argue and lose your temper
    b. Enjoy a good argument and keep your cool
    c. Avoid argument

14. Do you ever read a periodical that supports political views very different from yours?
    a. Never
    b. Sometimes, if you come across it
    c. Yes, you make a special effort to read it

15. Which statement do you most agree with?
    a. If crime were more severely punished, there would be less of it
    b. A better society would reduce the need for crime
    c. I wish I knew the answer to the problem of crime

16. Do you think
    a. That some rules are necessary for social living, but the fewer the better
    b. That people must have rules because they need to be controlled
    c. That rules are tyrannical

17. If you are a religious believer, do you think
    a. That your religion is the only right one
    b. That all religions have something to offer their believers
    c. That non-believers are wicked people

18. If you are not a religious believer, do you think
    a. That only stupid people are religious
    b. That religion is a dangerous and evil force
    c. That religion seems to do good for some people

19. Do you react to fussy old people with
    a. Patience and good humor
    b. Annoyance
    c. Sometimes a, sometimes b

20. Do you think the Women's Rights Movement is
    a. Run by a bunch of aggressive and insecure people
    b. An important social movement
    c. A joke

21. Would you marry someone of a different race?
    a. Yes
    b. No
    c. Not without thinking carefully about the various problems involved.

22. If your brother told you that he was a homosexual, would you
    a. Send him to a psychiatrist
    b. Feel shocked and accept him
    c. Feel shocked and reject him

23. When young people question authority, do you
    a. Feel uneasy
    b. Think that it is a good thing
    c. Feel angry

24. Which statement do you agree with
    a. Marriage is a bad institution
    b. Marriage is sacred and must be upheld
    c. Marriage is often difficult, but seems to meet the needs of many people

25. Do you think you are right in matters of belief rather than fact
    a. Always
    b. Often
    c. Rarely

26. If you stay in a household that is run differently from yours in matters of tidiness and regularity of meals, do you
    a. Fit in quite happily
    b. Feel constantly irritated by the chaos or the rigid orderliness of the place
    c. Find it fairly easy for a while, but not for too long

27. Do other people's personal habits annoy you
    a. Often
    b. Not at all
    c. Only if they are extreme or I am edgy

28. Which statement do you most agree with
    a. We should not judge other people's actions, because no one can ever fully understand the motives of another
    b. People are responsible for their actions and have to take the consequences
    c. Even if it is tough on some people, actions have to be judged

Check your scores

Question	a	b	c
1	4	2	0
2	4	0	2
3	4	0	4
4	4	0	2
5	0	4	2
6	0	0	4
7	0	2	4
8	4	0	2
9	4	2	0
10	4	2	0
11	0	4	2
12	4	2	0
13	4	0	2
14	4	2	0
15	4	2	0
16	0	4	4
17	2	0	4
18	4	4	0

19	0	4	2
20	4	0	4
21	0	4	2
22	2	0	4
23	2	0	4
24	4	0	2
25	4	0	2
26	0	4	2
27	4	0	2
28	0	4	2
Total			

Analysis Below 30

If your score lies in this range, you are a particularly cultural sensitive person. You are exceedingly aware of others' problems and difficulties and you have a natural capacity for accepting them even when they offend you. You will be a good friend and popular with others. You may find that other people abuse this sympathetic good nature because they have nothing to fear from recriminations. Even then, you are beyond reproach.

31-60

You are a culture sensitive person, and people will recognize you as one. If your score is above 50, however, you are probably sensitive and broad-minded in some areas only. Actually it is easy to be culturally sensitive if one does not hold very firm beliefs about anything. Look through the questions again and note where you picked up high rather than low scores. Were these questions in which personal comfort was directly concerned, or in which convictions or very strong ideological beliefs were touched upon?

61–89

You are not as culturally sensitive as many people, and if your score is higher than 80 you are basically an insensitive type of person. This will lead to clashes and short-term friendships. It will also mean that little things trouble you far more than they should and that you may waste emotional energy on what is really rather insignificant. It is very likely that you count yourself as someone with high principles, who tends to stick to important things rather than trivia. If you can get a wider experience of life and greater genuine contact with people, however, your will be more culturally sensitive, and in the end you will feel happier for it.

Over 90

This high score indicates that you are a very insensitive person. If your score is over 100, you are also bossy, self-opinionated, and quickly ~~to take~~ offended. You likely attract friends only interested in your money or generosity. If you really have scored this high, ask yourself why you are so unable to accept the faults in others. What are the aspects of other people that offend you most? Could it be that you are really punishing yourself for faults that you see in yourself".

Annual Diversity and Inclusion Plan of Action

To support you and your organization in your diversity and inclusion efforts we suggest the following weekly plan:

Week #	Quarter 1 (Actions / Plans)
Week 1	Write a diversity statement / vision that links to personal and / or organizational goals and objectives
Week 2	Create a measurement tool to assess progress towards your vision
Week 3	Assess the gap between your current state and your vision and rewrite the statement that your created in week 1 if needed
Week 4	Communicate with your team and / or family and friends your diversity vision and take their input into consideration
Week 5	Should you refine your statement and / or do you need to start having candid conversations with team / family
Week 6	Take action: Join a diversity council and / or a support group
Week 7	Create an action plan i.e. add diverse members to your team, link diversity to performance, have fun i.e. watch a diversity movie
Week 8	Research the value of diversity and inclusion in innovation and organizational development
Week 9	Train your team and / or yourself on being an inclusive leader. Discover your biases.

Week 10	Reflections: Reach out to someone you may have hurt (intentionally or unintentionally) by being culturally insensitive. Apologize.
Week 11	Celebrate differences within your team and / or treat yourself for this meaningful change
Week 12	Design a plan to outperform your competition by better understanding the diversity aspects of your customers

As you can tell the key purpose of this plan is to gather information and initiate action. In the second quarter of the year, the plan would evolve towards engagement and commitment:

Week #	Quarter 2 (Actions / Plans)
Week 14	Embrace a collaborative approach to your business and life i.e. suppliers, vendors, and your overall decisions
Week 15	Experience new hobbies, sports, activities, etc.
Week 16	Invest more in diversity and inclusion
Week 17	Envision a new future for yourself / family and for your team / organization

Week 18	Are you on LinkedIn, Tweeter, Facebook, Etc.? If not join and post about diversity
Week 19	Share an article on your social network sites about diversity
Week 20	Encourage your team and family to participate in diversity and inclusion activities
Week 21	Research the value of diversity and inclusion in innovation and organizational development and share with the world
Week 22	Try to reassign your team into new roles and / or new projects that are exciting to them i.e. base on their input
Week 23	Reflections: Reach out to someone you may have hurt (intentionally or unintentionally) by being culturally insensitive. Include them.
Week 24	Celebrate differences within your team and / or treat yourself for this meaningful change
Week 25	Assess your plan to outperform your competition. Modify as needed
Week 26	Assess your progress and improve your plans. Have you missed taking action in previous weeks? Why? What can be done differently?

In third and fourth quarters the plan moves to advocacy type of activities and it requires more efforts but the rewards for self, team, and the world could be significant.

Week #	Quarter 3 (Actions / Plans)
Week 27	Quantify and / or list the benefits of diversity and inclusion so far
Week 28	Challenge your team (and yourself) to come up with a disruptive strategy for the future
Week 29	Reach out to people you have never talked to / totally different parts of your company and / or approach new networks
Week 30	Reach out to someone totally different than you and engage them in candid conversations. Open your mind. Open your heart.
Week 31	Reflect on the past couple of weeks and share publically on LinkedIn, Facebook, Etc. what your open mind and heart have seen
Week 32	Support a diversity and inclusion cause outside your plan
Week 33	Encourage your team and family to participate in diversity and inclusion activities

Week 34	Research the value of diversity and inclusion in innovation and organizational development and share with the world
Week 35	Assess the new assignments of your team; how is it working? Any new learning? Do you need to course-correct?
Week 36	Seek constructive criticism from someone you trust. Encourage them to be candid and harsh if needed
Week 37	Celebrate differences within your team and / or treat yourself for this meaningful change
Week 38	Assess your plan to outperform your competition. Modify as needed
Week 39	Assess your progress and improve your plans. Have you missed taking action in previous weeks? Why? What can be done differently?

Week #	Quarter 4 (Actions / Plans)
Week 40	Create a diversity group and / or increase your involvement with your council that you joined in week 6
Week 41	Invite members to join your council
Week 42	Create a fund-raising plan to support diversity and inclusion

Week 43	Are you on track for your fund-raising event i.e. send more invitations, select different speakers, etc.
Week 44	Create a website for your diversity fund raising event
Week 45	Connect with your representative and discuss diversity and inclusion i.e. write a letter
Week 46	Fund raising event
Week 47	Share pictures and results on your website and social media
Week 48	Break
Week 49	Break
Week 50	Celebrate differences within your team and / or treat yourself for this meaningful change
Week 51	Assess your plan to outperform your competition. Modify as needed
Week 52	Assess your progress and improve your plans. Have you missed taking action in previous weeks? Why? What can be done differently?

Efforts alone doesn't yield results

Human Resources executives often scratch their head wondering about lack of diversity and inclusion in their organizations in spite tremendous efforts and resources to support diversity and inclusion let alone creating a culture of diversity and inclusion. The following case studies illustrate the point:

Case Study – Insurance Company

- The translation of the management diversity strategy to HRM activities is limited to activities concerning recruitment and selection.
- Focus on an increase of individuals with different cultural backgrounds, with these individuals expected to assimilate and adapt to the existing corporate culture without influencing it.
- In such a context, prejudice can continue to flourish under the surface.

Case Study – Telecommunication Company

- The diversity strategy seen as the way to make the most of all available talents and realize all potential.
- Newcomers made to feel welcome.
- Tolerance towards different perspectives and backgrounds rather than prejudice.
- Not yet a multicultural organization, even though its diversity management strategy aims in that direction.

Case Study – Bank

- Diversity management used primarily to attract ethnic customers to the bank, rather than to advance the quality of working life and career prospects of ethnic minority employees. The latter remain segregated in lower positions and not allowed to openly express their cultural and religious values.

Sound advices from different executives

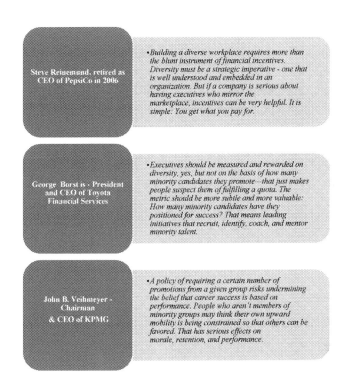

Figure 3 – Sound advices from different executives

Case Study:

Profile

After graduating from the University of Denver in 1981, Sharon Orlopp joined Footlocker where she worked her way up through the ranks from sales associate to become the Vice President of Human Resource Administration. Sharon joined Walmart in 2003 and was the Senior Vice President of Human Resources for Sam's Club, a division of Walmart, for eight years.

From 2011 to 2015, Ms. Sharon Orlopp served as the Global Chief Diversity Officer and Senior Vice President of Corporate Human Resources at Walmart. Ms. Orlopp's responsibilities included advancing a diverse workforce with 2.1 million associates worldwide. Ms. Orlopp has more than 30 years of management experience; 16 of those years have been spent in the human resources arena.

She has served on various boards including the Women's Foodservice Forum, Northwest Arkansas Radiation Therapy Institute, Enactus, and Future Business Leaders of America. Ms. Orlopp currently serves as a Board Member at The Harwood Institute and as an Advisory Board Member of her alma mater, the University of Denver, College of Arts, Humanities, and Social Sciences.

Your plan

As a Global Chief Diversity Officer, community activist, and business leader, Ms. Orlopp has tremendous insights to offer. In this case study we ask you (the reader of this book) to reflect on Ms. Orlopp's answers and incorporate the answers and your reflections into your personal approach towards becoming the inclusive leader:

1. In your opinion, why is diversity and inclusion important?

Diversity and inclusion are critical because they drive innovation. Different perspectives and experiences create unique ways to evaluate and solve business and world issues.

Creating an inclusive environment where all voices are heard and valued enables different solutions to be considered and implemented.

2. What are the similarities and differences, if any, between actions that should be taken by inclusive leaders at entry levels of supervision, mid-levels of management, and senior and executive levels of corporations to advance diversity and inclusion?

Inclusive behaviors should be demonstrated by all people at all times, irrespective of their position in the workplace, their community or in society. That being said, the "tone at the top" matters because employees and citizens often emulate behaviors they see leaders demonstrate. Leaders actions, words, behaviors, and decisions reflect their commitment to diversity and inclusion.

3. What are some of the common mistakes that leaders make while trying to advance diversity and inclusion?

Some of the common mistakes that leaders make while trying to advance diversity and inclusion are:

- Focusing solely or primarily on the numbers. Representation is important and metrics should be measured and shared regularly. Diversity without an inclusive environment typically causes retention issues for women, people of color, and underrepresented or marginalized groups.
- Believing that diversity will naturally occur. It is human nature to feel more comfortable with people

who are similar to you. Believing that diversity will naturally occur due to the changing demographics of the world doesn't ensure that diverse candidates will seek out, accept job offers, or stay with your company.

- Not having transparent, in-depth conversations. Creating safe environments for very honest, in-depth dialogue where employees can express their points of view and share personal stories can create discomfort, but it also generates personal growth and understanding. Using current event situations that have elements about diversity and inclusion are great topics to have transparent conversations about in order to learn from each other and to become knowledgeable about inclusion issues.

4. Some organizations house diversity teams within the human resource department while other organizations keep diversity as a stand-alone department. Some diversity and inclusion leaders report directly to the CEO (either as part of HR department or as an independent department) while other diversity and inclusion leaders report to EVP or Chief Human Resources Office. In your opinion, what structure is most effective and why?

There are a wide variety of responsibilities and reporting structures of Chief Diversity Officers. Many CDOs have responsibility for diversity and inclusion as well as other departments, such as sustainability, corporate social responsibility, ethics, culture, human resources, marketing, R&D.

Each company has unique organizational needs and each CDO has different skills and qualifications based on their past work experience. The magic occurs when companies can match a CDO's passion, skills, and expertise with key responsibilities within the organization.

What matters more than reporting structure or the other responsibilities of a CDO is the level of influence a CDO has within their organization and within the communities/regions the company supports.

5. Some diversity and inclusion strategies that were rolled out by several fortune 500 companies in the last few years ended up sounding and looking like marketing and PR campaigns. What is your perspective on this, and how can other companies avoid the trap of marketing diversity and inclusion vs. fully embracing diversity and inclusion?

The war for talent creates an insatiable need for talented people from all backgrounds. Companies genuinely want to have work environments where all employees thrive professionally and personally.

There isn't a "silver bullet" that effortlessly improves diversity and inclusion. It is a long term focus and strategy. It is a marathon, not a sprint.

Companies need to continually evaluate their diversity and inclusion efforts and results based on one year, three year, five year, and ten year increments. If diversity programs change regularly, measuring progress and assessing accountability becomes more challenging. Regular, frequent reporting about diversity and inclusion with senior management and the Board of Directors ensures that the focus remains on diversity and inclusion.

6. How should diversity and inclusion be measured in an organization?

There are a multitude of metrics that can be used to measure diversity and inclusion. I believe it is best to pick several core metrics that focus on three key areas: recruitment, retention, and advancement.

Key metrics in each of these areas include:

RECRUITMENT:

- New hire representation rates of women and people of color compared to existing representation rates. This provides a directional trend line indicator.

RETENTION:

- Retention rates of women compared to men
- Retention rates of people of color compared to whites
- Retention analytics that look at all the specific names of women and people of color over a specific time period to see if they are still employed. This helps highlight if there is a revolving door of hires and departures or if people are staying with the company.

ADVANCEMENT:

- Advancement rates of women compared to men
- Advancement rates of people of color compared to whites

Conclusion

Diversity and inclusion plays a key role in today's organization. Emerging realities, empirical research, and ethical arguments provide a solid case for diversity and inclusion. Diversity and inclusion is about empowerment of all people within an organization. It makes leaders and organizations more effective by capitalizing on the strengths of each employee by understanding, valuing, and using the differences in every person. It is important for leaders to reflect on the ethical case of diversity and engage in structured training to develop conscientious awareness about how to feel, think, and act to become "diverse leaders" and "diverse teams". Many diversity and inclusion efforts fail due to lack of deep and strategic commitment to diversity and inclusion coupled with the misconception that hiring more diverse people create diversity and inclusion.

The inclusive leader is distinguishable by his/her approach, style, and mindset. They are recognizable by the way they manage and lead. It takes efforts to move beyond biases, consciousness and unconsciousness, but training, including mentoring and mentorship, create awareness and action, key elements to developing the inclusive leader.

Organizations can develop diversity and inclusion by commitment i.e. strategic imperative of the organization that includes, incentives, diversity initiatives, mentorship, etc. as well as proper participatory training. In doing so, growth and rewards will naturally follow.

Chapter 3

LEADERSHIP AND CHANGE MANAGEMENT

A quick review of the history of organizations reveals that "change" is inevitable. To manage change, organizations employ different strategies to control and guide the journey toward long-lasting and improved organizational effectiveness.

Change Management

In 2006, O'Donovan provided four widely accepted basic definitions of change management: (1) the task of managing change, (2) an area of professional practice, (3) a body of knowledge, and (4) a control mechanism. According to Kritsonis, 2004, the concept of change management describes the processes for effecting change that moves individuals, groups, teams, organization, or societies from a current state of equilibrium to a different desired state.

Interventions in the process range greatly from the business model itself to structure and leadership. Some organizations focus on the human aspects of change or culture of the organization while other organizations focus on the process, structural and technological aspects. In most cases a combination of "engineered interventions" and "human interventions" define the overall design of change management. Consequently, there is no single strategy that definitely produces successful change management results; however, it is our experience that effective and lasting change requires complex approaches that include combinations of different tools, models, methods including incentives as well as effective leadership. Aside from the effectiveness, relevance, and proper designs or interventions, a key element for a successful change management is "buy-in" at all levels (i.e. honesty in providing feedback leading to proper design or intervention as well as execution of the change management process).

Many researchers argue that the discovery and development of Change Management theories stem from the practice of Organizational Psychology and its application to the fields of business and engineering. Within the human component of change, researchers differentiate between individual change and organizational change.

Individual Change: In 1951, Kurt Lewin developed one of the earliest models of change in which view individual change as a process that involves three steps. The first stage, *unfreezing,* involves the individual overcoming one's current attitude and behavior and dismantling the existing mindset. At the beginning of the process, status quo is the equilibrium status, and unfreezing is required to cause disequilibrium. During this step, it is critical for an individual to let self-guards down and open up to change so that altering one's mindset and changing behavior is not only possible but also acceptable.

In the second stage, *movement* or *change,* Kritsonis, 2004, argued it is necessary to move to a targeted new level of equilibrium. At this point, the individual may experience confusion due to the occurrence of change(s) taking place within. Purser and Petranker, 2005, explained that this confusion may occur because the individual's mindset is being challenged without any tangible or clear explanation to replace their original way of thinking.

The third stage, *refreezing,* Kritsonis, 2004, explained that it takes place after the change is implemented and is important in sustaining the change. In this stage, Purser and Petranker, 2005, elaborated the new mindset is gelling, a sense of new equilibrium is being realized, and the individual's comfort level is returning.

Needless to say, not all researchers agree with Lewin's three stages and the main criticism is the linear model that it adapts verses the complex and overlapping series of events that is often involved. Nevertheless, Lewin's paradigm provides a basic framework for conceptualizing change.

Organizational   Change: "Organizational Change Management" models describe the processes for managing the change of people at organizational levels. The concept of organizational change management is broad and includes various internal and external change process factors that influence change within an organization. Ford and Greer, 2006, summarized four organizational change process factors: (1) goal setting, (2) skill development, (3) feedback, and (4) management control.

Trends and Complexity of Change Management

Historically, according to Mastenbroek, 1996, we can see change management in early military maneuvers. During the sixteenth century the normal fighting group was a square fifty by fifty. This formation was the common method of fighting. Change management offered other formations that altered the shape to longer narrower formations; the organizational size did not change but the shape did, and the responsibilities of the members of the organization changed. Individuals became more important and consequently required more training. The next extension of this was the platoon where teamwork was a key component. As time progressed, change continued resulting in the military hierarchical bureaucracy.

Similarly, Hatch's (1997) different change methods carried over to the industrial revolution. With the development of factories and other establishments, the need for control, structure and organization grew. Early research shifted from more classical to modern with the focus to stabilize and increase productivity. Increases of various kinds seemed necessary to make improvements in organizations: more structure, more control, more of what had worked in the past. As organizations became more complex, ideas changed. As workers became more productive and better educated managers learned that they needed to motivate the workers. This resulted in the development of policy manuals, instruction manuals and job descriptions. It took time for managers to develop methods of working in special situations. If a job was necessary that did not work within the boundaries of the current organization, new plans were developed. If production required a specialist, leadership would determine how to incorporate the specialist into the organization. Mastenbroek, 2004, indicated that these special situations would generate a number of questions that required answers and decisions. Questions from a leader may include: Could they bring a specialist as a consultant and disrupt the current operation? If a specialist was necessary and invited, could they make the organization better?

Thus, Change Management is a highly complex phenomenon. Consequently, Living Systems Theory and Systems Thinking provide a foundation for understanding the complexities of Change Management. "Systems Thinking", a way of thinking about "Living Systems Theory", considers the interrelationships of the parts of a system to the whole system and the interdependence of the whole system to the parts. Flood, 2001, asserted that systems' thinking facilitates thinking about the interrelationships and interdependencies that exist among the parts of a system while simultaneously fostering thinking about and considering the wholeness of the system and the environment in which a system exists. A system is not merely the sum of its parts and the "whole is greater than the sum of its parts. Wheatley, 1999, explains:

> Each organism maintains a clear sense of its individual identity *within* a larger network of relationships that helps shape its identity. Each being is noticeable as a separate entity, yet it is simultaneously part of the whole system. While we humans observe and count separate selves, and pay a great deal of attention to the differences that seem to divide us, in fact we survive only as we learn how to participate in a web of relationships (p.20).

The pace of change in all types of organizations occurs at a phenomenally rapid rate. In 1992, Tyson reported that instability was the norm for most organizations. More recently, researchers and writers have concluded that the two greatest challenges facing organizations are both change and the leaders who are directing the response to change. While there is significant agreement among scholars and practitioners that the primary task of leaders is to bring about change by skilled leaders, there is little agreement on the methods whereby leaders might acquire the requisite skills to bring about successful change or the methods needed for change.

Change comes in various fashions: Emergent, planned, small, big, incremental, exponential, proactive, reactive, continuous, interval, discontinuous, reactive and anticipatory. As one might expect, different forms of change have engendered different forms of response.

In 2001, Coram and Burnes argued that contemporary trends support the idea that there is no one best way to address organizational change. To adopt one singular approach is to accept the logic that one approach is suitable for all organizations, in all situations and at all times. Clearly some entities function in turbulent environments while others operate in relatively stable conditions. Other varying characteristics of organizations support the conclusion that managers need to choose an approach that is suitable for their situation and in some situations, it may be necessary to combine, either concurrently or sequentially, different change approaches.

Change Management Models

Change occurs naturally and / or by design. We classify change into the following typology:

1) Natural.
2) Top-Down.
3) Transformational.
4) Strategic.
5) Mixed.

Natural change occurs under the pressure of reality and / or by the responses of shareholders, employees, customers, and business leaders to emergent realities. While some experts and consultants may neglect this type of change because change management is a "designed intervention", it is critical to understand the factors that shaped the organization and to recognize the forces that may drive and / or block "Change Management".

As the name implies, Top-down models start with the CEO, owner or president of the organization to initiate, support, and create change. In this model, the influence and commitment of the leader is the critical element to the success of the change process. The leadership determines all aspects of change including deciding the starting points, establishing the goals, the reward system, and accountability measures with, or without, consultation of works and shareholders. Workers' involvement or their voice is typically mute in this change model; success and failure is usually a leadership issue. The charisma, influence, authority, power, and leadership style of the leaders as those competencies relate to the reality of the organization and desired change plays a critical role in top-down change models.

Transformational Change created a shift in the business model, culture, structure, leadership styles, processes, and / or any other critical aspects of the organization i.e. drastically change the organization. This type of change occurs over a longer period of time and necessitates the "buy-in" of employees and shareholders. Without employees' buy-in, needed behavioral changes for the success of change at this magnitude may not occur. Shareholders may have to invest in the short run to acquire gains in the long run and without their buy-in financial support needed for change may dry out. Through buy-in by every level of the organization, this model succeeds when everyone participates and provides their support to the new model.

In *Transformational Change*, perhaps the most difficult element is cultural change. In 1992, Schein described corporate culture as having three levels: 1) artifacts, where culture is both enacted and reinforced through visible appearances and behaviors, such as physical layouts, dress codes, organizational structure, company policies, procedures and programs, and attitudes, 2) espoused values, where culture is manifested through belief and values and, 3) basic assumptions where culture is manifested through long-learned, automatic responses and established opinions. *Organizational Culture* is "the epicenter of change".

Strategic Change, designed to create a change in a department or departments such as Marketing, Human Resources, Operations, etc. (i.e. to drastically influence the organization). In 1996, Kotter proposed 8-step strategic change model that includes the following phases: 1) establish a sense of urgency; 2) create the guiding coalition; 3) develop a vision and strategy; 4) communicate the change vision; 5) empower employees for broad-based action; 6) generate short-term wins; 7) consolidate gains and produce more change; and, 8) anchor new approaches in culture. Other models may reduce the number of steps but cover the same conceptual areas.

As the name implies, Mixed Methods is a combination of change methods. In reality, it is difficult, if not impossible, for organizations especially large and complex organizations to confine change into one single method. Under the influence of people, uncertainty, and unpredictability organizations speed up, expand, slowdown, and even alter change designs. The authors believe that successful Change Management must be flexible enough to respond to changing realities and perhaps a mixed method is the best design in reality.

Regardless of the Change Management type and model that is being developed, it is important to understand some of the inherit problems of change. In 1996, Michael Heifetz and Stan Halle summarized some of the common change management problems, which include:

- There is not enough dissatisfaction with the status quo.
- The vision is not fully developed or compelling enough.
- The vision neither owned nor translated into action by the people who must make the change work.
- Strong leadership is lacking; the leadership coalition is not powerful enough or lacks alignment.
- Political opposition can disrupt or destroy a change effort if left unchecked.

By knowing these issues, a leader should be able to come up with a plan that addresses each area and develop solutions to overcome them in kind. As Sun Tzu's *The Art of War* states: "know your enemy".

The next step in moving the organization in the desired direction is to develop the change plan. In 1993, Emily Gilbert and Brian H Kleiner provided 5 activities, which contribute to effective Change Management:

1. The motivation of change.
2. The creation of a vision.
3. The development of political support.
4. The management of the transition.
5) The sustaining of the momentum.

Developing the Change Management Leader

Leading change is an art and a science. We argue that change efforts fail due to leadership failures in one way or another. Even when failure is the result of the "change design" or "change plan" it is a leadership failure. However, *Change Management* success requires more than sound leadership and sound technical advice. To illustrate, see the following case study on Home Depot's story of *Change Management*.

Case Study – Change at the Home Depot the Nardelli Style

In 2006, Ram Charan posed the question:

What could be harder than turning around a seemingly wildly successful company by imposing a centralized framework on a heretofore radically decentralized, anti-establishment, free-spirited organization?

Seemingly a successful company, the fastest growing in retail history, Home Depot was facing what similar successful companies face: Growing the business at a faster rate than growing its people, taking short cuts and neglecting processes to achieving quick results, and covering deep legal, cultural, and business wounds by bandages. Taking the organization from a $40 billion "start up" company to a $100 billion global corporation within 5 years required "transformational change" under some legendary leadership.

As a successful GE executive, Bob Nardelli became the CEO of The Home Depot replacing popular founders Bernie Marcus and Arthur Blank, both in their 50s at the time, to specifically transform the Home Depot. Nardelli hired a colleague from GE, Dennis Donovan, as Home Depot's head of Human Resources. Donovan and Nardelli started their change efforts by formalizing and standardizing the corporate culture where data replaced intuition in decision-making, and specific performance criteria and metrics replaced gut-feel and spontaneous approach to performance reviews. Six Sigma replaced "Stack it high and watch it fly". Within 5 years, two amazing things happened:

1) Successfully, the organization more than doubled its earnings per share and became $80 billion organization.
2) Surprisingly, share price dropped from $70 in the late 1990s to $20 in 2003.

In 2007, Bob Nardelli resigned from the Home Depot under controversial circumstances. Nardelli's severance package estimated at $210 million. His successor was Frank Blake, the Home Depot vice chairman and executive vice president, who also worked closely with Nardelli at GE.

Many would argue that Nardelli's sudden resignation and departure represented a failure to change management efforts at The Home Depot. As a District Manager with the Home Depot at the time, the first author of this book argues the opposite. Granted, in hindsight the process of change could have been different but overall Home Depot was changed as an organization, grew as a business, and today, the organization remains the number one home improvement company in the world.

As a leader, Nardelli had some of the best consultants in the world to guide his decisions including Ram Charan. So, the successes and disappointments that he brought and encountered are great lessons to evolving change management leaders.

Successes

As witnessed by the first author and summarized by Ram Charan, among the tools Home Depot have used are:

1) Data templates, detailed forms to organize performance data for quarterly business review meetings, which encourage personal accountability, give employees a deeper understanding of business performance, and foster collaboration by putting people on the same page when making decisions.

2) Strategic Operating and Resource Planning, or SOAR, which is built around an annual eight-day session when Home Depot's 12 top executives work together to balance priorities and select the investments most likely to achieve financial and other business targets.

3) Disciplined talent reviews, conducted frequently, and consistently from one to the next, which

emphasize the need for candor and fairness in dealing with employee performance.

4) Store manager learning forums that, through role playing, simulations, and other exercises, highlighted the level of competitive threats and made transparent the company's future plans, helping attendees understand the need for the new strategy.

5) Monday morning conference calls, involving the company's top 15 executives, during which accountability (for business results and for promises made the previous week) is emphasized, as is sharing information (about operations, customers, markets, and competitive conditions).

6) Employee task forces, staffed by individuals from all levels of the company, to elicit unfiltered input from the people closest to a problem and gain their support for the changes the solution requires.

7) An array of leadership development programs, including the Future Leaders Program, the Store Leadership Program, and the Merchandising Leadership Program, which raise the bar for performance and ensure continuity of the culture.

8) Mapping of the HR process, which identified 300 ways that HR tasks improved and highlighted the importance of instituting processes to sustain cultural change.

Disappointments

From Nardelli's perspective one would wonder about three fundamental questions:

1) For a company that doubles its earnings per share within 5 years and achieve what it did in the previous 25 years, why on earth didn't the stock price react positively to those impressive financials?
2) In a capitalist society, does it really matter how much a person legally and contractually earns?
3) Resistance to change is normal and expected but "fierce resistance" for a change and a leader who was brought in by the founders is incomprehensible.

Buy-in of followers to change efforts remains one of the most important aspects of successful change management. In depth understanding of the technical aspects and operations of the organization is also critical to success. Take the perception that customer service declined at the Home Depot under Nardelli, for example. In reality, Nardelli wanted to offer customers safer conditions and improved services. Prior to Nardelli, Home Depot employees moved dangerous loads of lumber, concrete, and heavy doors during shopping hours and within an 8-month period, 3 people died at the Home Depot due to unsafe practices. In November 1999, Mary Margaret Penturff and her daughter stopped by their local Home Depot in Santa Monica to buy lattice for their patio. A 75-pound box of wood fell from a shelf above the 79-year-old Penturff, leaving her bleeding on the sales floor with a fatal head wound. Six months later, on a Memorial Day weekend, the Horner family went to their local Home Depot store in Twin Falls, Idaho, to shop and more than 2,000 pounds of kitchen countertops fell about 10 feet from a forklift that was moving them, hitting their 3-year-old daughter, Janessa. She died four hours later at a local hospital. Two months after that, Jerry Mead, 41, and his brother were shopping in a Home Depot store in

Danbury, Connecticut, when they were hit by 2,000 pounds of falling landscaping timbers. Jerry Mead died and his brother seriously injured.

So prior to Nardelli, stores had customers and employees everywhere in the store operating simultaneously in a dangerous environment. Nardelli decided to focus on overnight operations and move resources / heavy lifting to overnight when customers were not shopping to allow employees faster and safer movement and to protect customers during daytime from potential hazards of operations. However, shifting resources away from customers' eyes gave the perception that Home Depot is severely cutting service. Granted, Home Depot could have made certain moves to minimize and / or negate the negative consequences of shifting resources but those who resisted change focused on some of the negative consequences of change instead of thinking creatively of overcoming certain obstacles that may come with change.

Among the tools that leaders should use while leading change, we recommend:

1) People / frontline employees should be involved in the process of change. No involvement, no buy-in. No buy-in to execution.
2) Change should look and feel like bottom-up not top-down especially in large organizations.
3) Winning the hearts of the organization is perhaps more important than winning the minds of the organization. Effective leaders are usually rational and due to the pressure of reality they have little room for emotions. However, more important than providing a sound case for change is winning peoples' hearts not only for the 'idea of needed

change' (usually people see it and know it) but more so capturing their attention and hearts upon introducing the new idea or concept.

4) Always ask: What are the potential negative consequences of change on all those who are involved: customers, vendors and business partners, employees, and shareholders. Create a mitigating plan and most importantly create actions to minimize or preferably eliminate those negative consequences.

5) Anticipate fierce resistance to change especially when attached to the way people work and / or when change appears to jeopardize jobs. For example, when Nardelli introduced Six Sigma to the Home Depot, some employees were probably intimidated and terrified of position replacement possibilities by those who know Six Sigma. Nardelli's intention was to train employees on a new skill that is beneficial for the organization and for employees. However, the naysayers rushed to oppose Six Sigma and declare that what worked for Nardelli in the industrial setting of GE will not work in the service setting of the Home Depot.

6) The more fundamental the change needed, may require an allocation of more time and resources.

7) Define what success looks like and monitor progress against time and budget.

Chapter 4

COLLABORATIVE SERVANT LEADERSHIP AS AN EFFECTIVE LEADERSHIP MODEL

While the roots of servant leadership are deep in human history, it was not until 1970 when Robert K. Greenleaf proposed Servant Leadership as a theoretical framework and as a form of leadership where a leader's primary motivation and role was to serve others. The core argument of this model is that serving followers have a positive impact; thus inspiring followers to do more collectively, as a cohesive team, than they would do individually as disconnected workers. In 1996, Larry Spears, defined servant-leadership as:

…A new kind of leadership model – a model which puts serving others as the number one priority. Servant-leadership emphasizes increased service to others; a holistic approach to work; promoting a sense of community; and the sharing of power in decision-making (p. 33).

In most cases, servant leaders possess an exemplary amount of charisma. Charismatic leaders are usually able to energize others by their own self-energy, drive commitment and action by their unwavering set of beliefs and relentless pursuit of a vision. Servant leaders are caring individuals and typically put the needs of others first which is a clear distinction from dictators and / or selfish leaders who put their own personal agenda and status first. Other traits include:

Listen to employees and constantly check the office climate: Leaders that solicit feedback, advice, and listen to the collective wisdom and tribal knowledge of their employees understand the importance of communication and listening as a powerful management tool. Employees need to feel that their opinions and experiences matter to leadership in the organization. Servant-leader gain understanding of the pulse, climate, and character of the organizational culture. Listening also includes being reflective and listening to one's inner voice as it relates to decision making and leading others.

Show compassion, concern, and empathy for the well-being of others: Servant leaders strive to understand and empathize with the challenges, issues, and problems of others. Employees need to be recognized and accepted for their contribution. Their special circumstances should also be understood and considered.

Assist with healing by promoting a nurturing and supportive environment: Often when new leaders take over, there are existing employees with open wounds from neglect, poor management, organizational conflict, or unexpected structural changes. Learning to help others move on, accept change, and heal is an important aspect of servant leadership.

Understand their employees' strengths, limitations, and needs: Servant leaders have the ability to understand and be aware of employees'– management barriers, organizational challenges, and their own person shortcomings.

Influential, positive and persuasive: Servant leaders depend on persuasion not positional authority. They explain the benefits and the purpose of actions; they don't coerce nor do they hide behind "compliance" and "regulations". This particular aspect offers clear distinctions between traditional dictatorship style and that of servant leadership. The servant leader is effective at building loyalty, followership, and consensus within organizational culture and across organizational departments and boundaries.

Show conceptualization, vision, and know how to articulate in a manner that excites and inspires others: Servant leaders seek to nurture their abilities to imagine greatness and dream enormous dreams from a strategic / big picture perspective that focuses on the huge rewards of success and not on the fear of failure. This includes finding the delicate and sometimes difficult balance between the big picture / strategy and the day to day operational needs / tactics.

Show foresight on a consistent basis: Foresight is a trait that enables servant leaders to take risks and to learn from failures in a way that focuses on finding value in what went wrong and not on finding individuals to blame for mistakes.

It is about the ability to positively apply lessons learned in the past to impact the present and shape the future. This often means having the courage, sense of urgency, and inclination to swift interventions to change a course of action if results / trends steered in the wrong direction.

Work to gain trust: Effective servant leaders are ethical. They take personal and unselfish ownership of situations and consequences. They show character, trustworthiness, responsibility, social responsibility, and accountability for their actions and decisions. They are willing to trust others, blindly if needed as part of their developed "judgment" especially judgment of character and people.

Show sincere commitment to developing and growing of others: Servant leaders are passionate about helping employees see the potential of their talents and skills. They are committed to helping remove the unnecessary organizational roadblocks that hinder employees' growth and development. They understand the value and importance of professional development and organizational development as critical to creating an organizational culture that can adapt and respond effectively to expected and unexpected change.

Remove obstacles: Servant leaders must foresee obstacles that prevent success but most importantly they must remove them. Servant leaders facilitate for the team what the team cannot do individually.

Community builders: Servant leaders understand they must foster a climate that encourages a sense of partnership, teamwork, and community. Consequently, employees collaborate, pool collective knowledge, and develop cohesiveness towards common goals that benefit the organization and the community.

Servant leadership in practice is about operational principle that values the responsibilities, interests, and abilities of all affected parties, and actively encourages inclusive involvement in planning and decision-making through reflection and study, collective actions, and open discussion toward consensus. A servant leader serves as he or she leads, and who in turn garners support by a mass of constituents who work similarly as hard to carry out major themes. To that end, servant leaders create a field of influence that stimulates experiential organizational learning, perspective reflection, critical thinking, empowerment, pooling of collective wisdom, and encourages a climate for active and inclusive participation and creative innovations through collective analysis (Simonaitiene, Leonaviiene, & Zvirdauskas, 2004).

Servant Leadership in Action

In "real life" action and results matter the most. The question that faces students of leadership and executives in leadership training sessions is how to translate ideas and lessons of leadership into actions and results in the workplace. This chapter provides specific research methodology and specific examples to translate ideas of leadership into action and results in "real life". Although the lessons are retail industry driven, the approach is applicable to most "real life" situations.

A Roadmap for Execution – Evidence from the Retail Industry

Sutton (2004: 2) argued that the most universally asked, researched, and debated question among management practitioners and academics, is "what is the most effective style of leadership"? The previous sections of this book provided conceptual answers and this section provides a practical answer from the retail industry. The retail industry and its critical position to the US economy was a deliberate choice. According to recently published US data, the retail industry continues to be the second-largest industry in the United States both in number of establishments and number of employees, accounting for over one million establishments and 11.6 percent of the total U.S. employment with over 15.6 million people (US Bureau of Labor Statistics, 2008), and sales' estimates edging toward $4.4 trillion (US census bureau, 2009). However, it is surprising that very limited research tackles leadership attributes of successful managers in the retail industry exist in spite the fact that Retail Store Managers are the key driving force behind a retail firm's profit (Shim, Lusch, Goldberry, 2002). Indeed, when scholarly journals were searched using the ProQuest search engine with the term Myers-Briggs Type Indicator in the citation and abstract, 176 papers were retrieved. However, when this search was refined by the term "retail" in the "citation and abstract", only two papers were rendered. Even when wider search terms than "Myers-Briggs" were used, (i.e. personality type and retail, in citation and abstract), the search retrieved similar trends as indicated by Table 1, which clearly illustrates that while leadership and managerial skills are widely researched, tackling leadership attributes and retail store managers is still in a very nascent stage.

Terms Searched	Leadership & Managerial Skills	Leadership & Personal Profiles	Leadership & Chief Executive Officers	Leadership & Retailing Industry	Leadership & Store Managers
No. of Articles Found	753	280	355	19	12

Table 1 – ProQuest Search Results

Nevertheless, available research appears to raise many questions and limited answers. For example, Pittenger (2005) found that multiple researchers concluded that managers who balance competing leadership roles tend to be more successful than those who display a specific leadership function (Hooijberg, 1996; Quinn, 1988; Quinn et al., 1991; Hart and Quinn, 1993). However, other researchers concluded that certain leadership styles are more essential than others for effective leadership (Shamir et al., 1993; Sosik et al., 1997). In a very interesting study, Nicholson and Cushman (2000) found that there is a significant communication gap between industry and the academics as to what is important for success in the retailing field. For example, Nicholson and Cushman (2000) found that retail industry respondents rated strong affective characteristics very highly, such as "ability to deal with conflict", "leadership" and "decision making", but academic respondents, on the other hand, rated two cognitive skills very highly, "understanding of company's business environment" and "product knowledge" plus more interpersonal affective attributes such as "customer service focus" and "ability to work as a team". Lindblom, Olkkonen, and Mitronen (2008) investigated the cognitive styles of contractually integrated retail entrepreneurs with respect to marketing decision making and found no clear relationship between the cognitive styles of the respondents and their business performance. Pittenger (2005) confirmed that the shared variance between a personality dimension and work performance is 4%. Therefore, those who claim a link between personality and performance must acknowledge that the majority of work performance reflects many other influences. Furthermore, Pittenger (2005) recommended that future research that examines the predictive power of personality tests should incorporate other measures of performance, including intelligence, knowledge and experience, and skill. Interestingly, Ayad (2008) conducted a case study that integrated the principles of action research and traditional qualitative research and concluded that success in retail at a store level is a function of "critical thinking, inspirational leadership, and functional knowledge" regardless of personality types and other factors.

CASE STUDY

The case study is based on Ayad's (2008) research. The following sections are arranged to describe an issue, context, action, and / or lessons which supports aspects of servant leadership.

The issue: inventory management

Inventory optimization is a major challenge not only for retailers and manufacturers, but also for the US Government. A study by the Government Accountability Office (GAO, 2005) concluded that the department of defense (DOD), does not have effective management processes, systems, and controls in place to assure that it is reutilizing excess inventory to the maximum extent possible and safeguarding excess items from damage, loss, and theft, as required by federal regulations, DOD policy, and GAO internal control standards. As a result, the study found substantial waste and inefficiency related to DOD's excess property reutilization program. Of the $18.6 billion in reported fiscal year 2002 and 2003 excess commodity disposals, $2.5 billion related to items in new, unused, and excellent condition (A condition). Of the $2.5 billion, the study determined that $2.2 billion included substantial waste and inefficiency because new, unused, and excellent condition items transferred or donated outside of DOD, sold on the internet for pennies on the dollar, or destroyed rather than recycled. The study also found that DOD purchased at least $400 million of identical commodities instead of reutilizing available A-condition excess items (GAO, 2005, p. 4).

Manufacturers and retailers face similar challenges with excess inventory. In early 2006, Wal-Mart announced plans to cut inventory by $6 billion in 100 days; and Charles Holley, Wal-Mart Senior Vice President said "Inventory is playing a big part in return on investment. . . As we become more market relevant. . . you'll see inventory will still have a ways to go down" (Cassidy, 2006). Estimates of excess inventory vary widely. A survey by AMR Research projected that the excess consumer goods inventory would exceed $60 billion in the USA and $120 billion globally at the end of 2000 (Frozen Food Age, 2000). The survey of 165 manufacturers and retailers found that 4 percent of the $1.3 trillion in sales from manufacturers to distributors and retailers was excess inventory. Evaluating 20-inventory profiles from companies in different business sectors, Relph and Barrar (2003) estimated between 10 and 98 percent of the inventory values were "in overage".

Like excess inventory, Out of Stock (OOS), could be very costly as well. According to Gruen and Corsten (2006) worldwide OOS levels still average 8 percent. And for every 13 items a shopper plans to purchase, one will be OOS. For promoted items, OOS levels hover at 16 percent, or one OOS item for every seven promoted items a shopper plans to purchase. Furthermore, the gaps on shelves are costing retailers up to 4 percent of sales. When confronted with a shelf-level OOS, on average 30 percent of consumers switch stores; 25 percent switch brands and 20 percent switch to a lower-value alternative" (Gruen and Corsten, 2006). An average customer may not return to a store after three negative experiences and Wal-Mart estimates that each lost customer represents over $200,000 in lifetime lost sales (RRilley, 2004). If one assumed that a home owner would replace main items and structures such as roofing, siding, doors, windows, flooring, basement remodeling, kitchen, bath, appliances, etc. in his or her home once in a lifetime, such a loss could easily exceed $100,000 per customer for the home improvement industry.

The Lesson: Ownership

Servant leaders identify meaningful opportunities for their teams or organizations (vision / foresight) and tackle them successfully. They take ownership (to remove obstacles) and the "opportunity" of the team becomes their personal commitment (sincerity).

The Inquiry: Exploration with Store Managers

The leader started a collaborative inquiry by creating an open dialogue with store managers, his team, around top most important projects for them. Ironically, seven store managers, operating seven different locations ranging in sales between $20 and $45 million or so had similar priorities. Interestingly, one of their top focuses was inventory; a traditional focus for retail organizations. For that, the team reviewed available data and noticed significant variations in inventory results between stores. For example, out of 11 selling departments, one department in one store had two OOS as indicated by the system; and the same department in another store had 30 OOS.

Verifying the data visually, a similar percentage of variation existed. Stabilizing the variations and optimizing the results represented our ultimate goal. Thus, the team's mission became to drop those two OOS to zero or at least to stabilize stores at two OOS in this department in every store if these OOS were due to factors outside the control of stores such as logistics, imports, etc. In the meantime, the team decided to drive 100 percent execution on our business practice to ensure that no customer leaves their stores unhappy even if we had to upgrade customers to the next level at the same original price.

The Lesson: Communication / Support / Vision

The leader initiated a collaborative inquiry to gather "buy-in" because involvement and commitment go hand and hand. The leader envisioned improving best results and / or realistically working with the team for all to achieve the result of the best member store (inclusiveness). The leader understood what the team can and cannot control. Focusing on what the team controls makes expectations realistic and reduces frustrations that comes with unattainable results.

The Goals: Key Measurements

By consensus, this team selected optimizing inventory levels as their collaborative project. The team established two holistic improvement objectives related to inventory:

1. Reduce total inventory levels.
2. Maximize availability of inventory from customers' point of view, (i.e. the right product in the right location with enough quantities for customers' specific requirements).

In order to sell a product quickly and satisfactory, not only it has to be in the store, but also it needs to be in its correct location, (i.e. not on the overhead or backrooms). In addition, the team established the following goals with specific percentages:

3. Reduce slow moving inventory.
4. Reduce clearance inventory.
5. Improve the process of ordering, receiving, packing-out from receiving to overheads and homes, and packing-down from overheads to homes. This includes organizing overheads.
6. Improve the process of products' markdown to achieve broader goals including preventive measures, i.e. reduced markdowns due to damage.
7. Ensuring availability of "whole-project quantities" while reducing inventory.

The Lessons: Clarity and Specificity

Servant leaders understand that vagueness creates uncertainty, divisions, and frustrations. They also keep the end in mind. And they deeply believe that achieving goals is the fuel of inspiration and energy.

Cycles of Action and Reflection: Engagement

After establishing consensus on the project and its specific goals, the leader's role shifted to provide empowerment, encouragement, support, follow up, and recognition so that the entire team acts to create learning and improvements. Furthermore, the leader acted as the facilitator of critical communications. The role of store managers was to design and execute specific plans that match their individual situations. The team decided that the theory of one solution fits all stores does not work because each store has its own personality, its own strengths, and its own environmental challenges. Not surprisingly, internal and external factors contributed to the speed of improvements and progress towards results.

Team's cycles of action and reflection are summarized as follows:

1. Take action towards established goals, and reflect on these actions seeking better results daily;
2. Review and assess previous week's results individually, i.e. store managers alone, one-on-one with me, and as a team on weekly conference calls and e-mails;
3. Identify successes and opportunities;

4. Share practices that led to successes and opportunities;
5. Compare and contrast improvement practices;
6. Celebrate successes; and
7. Create new actions and targets for improvements.

The Lessons: Engagement is when Servant Leadership is Most Needed

The core aspects of servant leadership (empowerment, encouragement, support, care to follow up, care for wellbeing of individuals as well as results, and recognition to inspire even higher results leading to learning and improvements) are critical during the engagement stage. While servant leaders are always engaged, it is when action is taken their qualities are needed the most. As stated earlier, results are the soul of organizations. Most leaders understand that; in fact, in today's organizations getting results is the most basic requirement of leadership. Consequently, in the heat of the battle, some leaders forget about the team, care, compassion, etc. and focus on results. In their mind, results will solve it all. But so often while driven by their high personal energy to achieve results they may commit critical mistakes such as not listening, not paying attention, not caring, not trusting, etc.

Engagement: But where are the Results?

In a one-on-one reflection between the leader and one team members exploring a situation that showed the slowest improvements, the manager assured the leader that his team was at the top of the situation; not only the results would soon follow, he emphasized, they would exceed other locations. So, with confidence the leader and managers called this team for a meeting. After all, reports indicated improvements. When the store manager and the leader started asking specific and deep questions related to the project, it became clear that many answers were either wrong or incomplete. Finally, the store manager and the leader realized reasons some results were not up to par. Training and communication were clear opportunities for improvement in this specific case. In addition, the meeting revealed hidden stress and confusion because this particular location made some shuffling between team members and roles but leaders of this business unit underestimated the team's dissatisfaction with the change and its consequences.

The Lessons: Managing Perceptions

In this case, the stunning fact was the "doers", i.e. players who make things happen told a different story than managers. Disengaged leaders look at the reports in isolation of situations, however reports only show numbers but they do not show emotions nor do they show true picture of the situation. Let alone its true long-term consequences. When the leader repeated the same approach randomly in different locations, to leader's surprise the answers were not a lot better than the previous ones. Consequently, it is vital to realize the critical nature of "context" on "real life" situations. Employees who may have a good functional knowledge appear to be comfortable and relaxed which is a positive factor but too much relaxation and reliance on the artistic repertoire can result in inferior outcomes in certain situations; similarly, lack of functional knowledge also resulted in inferior outcomes. As the leader identifies issues, the journey continues.

Results: "Real Life"

The cycles of action and reflection within "servant leadership context" worked and rendered excellent results. After only two weeks of this process, 100 percent of the managers improved their in-stock position and 57 percent of managers exceeded goals. Before the beginning of this process, the team was almost 5 percent over (worse than) established goals in inventory levels, and after six weeks the team actually exceeded (better than) the goal by 2.1 percent. Furthermore, at the beginning one location was over inventory goal by over 10 percent, while another location was 3 percent over goal. This gap was improved and reduced between 1.0 and 3.9 percent. However, the location that reduced inventory to 3.9 percent under inventory goal experienced increased amounts of OOS. Ironically, another store was 3 percent under inventory goal and significantly in a high in stock position. Thus, we established a new goal to take all locations to that optimal goal of 3 percent under initial inventory goal with zero OOS whenever possible. Overall, the speed and consistency of improvements were impressive, but most importantly the lessons that the teams shared, learned, and gained forever were the most valuable return an employer would hope for.

The Lessons: Simplicity and Complexity of Servant Leadership

Based on leader's academic and professional repertoire, and this collaborative inquiry i.e. case study, it can be argued that retail success at field level is simply a function of translating effective decisions into timely actions and executions at maximum productivity. In turn, this is a function of critical thinking (CT), functional knowledge, and leadership. To further clarify the role of leadership, the leader of this inquiry wrote:

> "The most important aspect of big box retail leadership is its ability to energize others through actions, ideas, and words... This leadership is more than charismatic leadership as it extends its wings to identify talent, grow talent, trust, empower, and follow up on commitments. Furthermore, it is the ability to create an environment of candor, responsibility, and respect. It is about creating a balance between accountability and inspiration, courageously confronting reality and consistently building relationships. It encompasses strategic planning and tactical implementation. Leaders display true emotions when appropriate, and contain frustrations when needed. They help others see the vision, the future, and the possibilities so that what seems initially impossible becomes possible. This leadership is not a dreaming or imaginary endeavor because it is reality based. In this expedition, reality becomes the subject of thinking, reflection-learning, and improvements not the constraint of innovation and change." (Ayad, 2008)

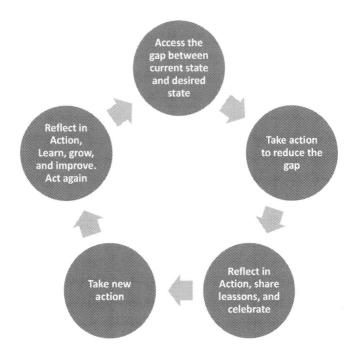

Figure # 1 – The cycles of action, reflection-in-action, improvements, and results

Conclusion

This chapter provided a specific example and a roadmap for translating ideas of this book into results in the "real life". It is critical to note that there is no "silver bullet" with effective leadership. People, situations, technologies, environment, societies, balance of power, etc. change consistently, and leaders must anticipate and respond to future trends. Servant leadership and / or inclusive leadership are not "boxed" concepts or "checklists". Leadership is a living body with a miraculous soul i.e. things to do (body and construct of leadership) and vital aspects such as servitude and integrity (soul of leadership). Perhaps the best way to understand the body and soul of effective leadership is to live it in action. We invite you to practice the principles of "inclusive leadership" as described in this book within your sphere of influence every day.

Chapter 5

LEADERSHIP TOOLS & TEAM BUILDING

In the previous chapter we illustrated a practical way to translate the concepts of servant leadership as an effective leadership model into action and results in the "real world". In this chapter, we will provide tools and explanations that help developing attributes that are vital to effective leadership.

Critical Thinking

As a result of variations in the theories and definitions of Critical Thinking, CT, American Philosophical Association assigned Peter Facione, in 1987, to head a systematic inquiry into research on critical thinking. Facione and a panel of experts representing several academic disciplines formed the "Delphi Project". One outcome of this project was a definition of CT. The panel's consensus statement regarding the definition of CT and the Ideal Critical Thinker states:

We understand critical thinking to be purposeful, self-regulatory judgment which results in interpretation, analysis, evaluation, and inference, as well as explanation of the evidential, conceptual, methodological, criteriological, or contextual considerations that form our judgment. CT is essential as a tool of inquiry. As such, CT is a liberating force in education and a powerful resource in one's personal and civic life. While not synonymous with good thinking, CT is a pervasive and self-rectifying human phenomenon. The ideal critical thinker is habitually inquisitive, well-informed, trustful of reason, open-minded, flexible, fair minded in evaluation, honest in facing personal biases, prudent in making judgments, willing to reconsider, clear about issues, orderly in complex matters, diligent in seeking relevant information, reasonable in the selection of criteria, focused in inquiry, and persistent in seeking results which are as precise as the subject and the circumstances of inquiry permit. Thus, educating good critical thinkers means working toward this ideal. It combines developing CT skills with nurturing those dispositions which consistently yield useful insights and which are the basis of a rational and democratic society (Facione, 1990, p. 2).

The above definition is one of the most comprehensive definitions that the authors could find. For the purpose of this book and for practicality, it is important to simplify the definition into its main components as follows:

1. Judgment.
2. Evidence.
3. Biases.
4. Knowledge.
5. Humility.

Think about the above 5 terms and answer the following questions:

1. How do I create options and alternatives to solve problems?
2. How do I analyze data?
3. What are my biases? How am I preventing my biases to influence my decisions?

Data Analysis

Statistical analysis is very important to sound decisions, but most importantly Effective Leaders are able to critically understand the meaning and reasonability of data. To illustrate, Best (2001) cites the following quotation "Every year since 1950, the number of American children gunned down has doubled" and states:

> Accepting these data without CT leads to mistakes, as the statement is "impossible". What makes this statistic so bad? Just for the sake of argument, let's assume that "the number of American children gunned down" in 1950 was one. If the number

doubled each year, there must have been two children gunned down in 1951, four in 1952, eight in 1953, and so on. By 1960, the number would have been 1,024. By 1965, it would have been 32,768 (in 1965, the F.B.I. identified only 9,960 criminal homicides in the entire country, including adult as well as child victims). By 1970, the number would have passed one million; by 1980, one billion (more than four times the total US population in that year). Only three years later, in 1983, the number of American children gunned down would have been 8.6 billion (nearly twice the earth's population at the time). Another milestone would have been passed in 1987, when the number of gunned-down American children 137 billion would have surpassed the best estimates for the total human population throughout history 110 billion. By 1995, when the article was published, the annual number of victims would have been over 35 trillion; a really big number of a magnitude you rarely encounter outside economics or astronomy.

The original statistics came from the Children's Defense Fund, a well-known advocacy group for children. The CDF's The State of America's Children Yearbook (1994) details: "The number of American children killed each year by guns has doubled since 1950." Note the difference in the wording. The CDF claimed there were twice as many deaths in 1994 as in 1950; the quotation reworded that claim and created a very different meaning.

As a result, a recommendation of formal training in algebra and statistics joined the definition of effective leadership. Granted, not all decisions require data analysis but most businesses and organizations need adequate business analysis, and effective leaders need to relay on facts; both qualitative and quantitative.

Exercise:

Look at the most recent decision that you made. Did you base your decision on data and / or fact? If so, how do you know that your data is accurate? Was the inference statistically and / or logically valid?

Decision Making

Think about your best personal or business decision / action. Answer the following questions:

1. What criteria did you use to choose the decision?
2. How did you make the outcome happen?
3. Did you receive any help and / or support from anyone? If yes, who did help you? Why did they help you? How are you going to thank them?
4. Did you receive any help and / or support from anyone? If no, how would the outcome be if you had some support? Why didn't you seek support? For the next big decision, how are you going to get support?

Role-Model

Think about the best leader (or teacher, family member, etc.) you've ever had / encountered. Reflect and answer the following:

1. Why did you like this specific leader the most?
2. How did your selected leader improve the business / class / family / etc.?
3. Describe your feelings when you talked and / or listened to your top leaders. What did you do about what you heard / saw?

Meetings

Think about a time when you attended a productive meeting. For all of those who were in the meeting. Answer the following:

1. What were the factors that made the meeting productive?
2. How did you measure the productivity of the meeting?
3. How can you make your meetings more productive?
4. How are you going to measure the gap between productivity expectations and actual productivity?

Performance Management

Think about the development plan that you've created for yourself; answer the following questions:

1. Does your plan take organizational objectives or needs into consideration? If yes, state the specific

objectives. If not, select specific organizations (or corporate) objectives that you may tie into your personal development plan (PDP).

2. Select your top 1-2 strengths and decide on how you are going to leverage your strengths.

3. Select a "developmental leadership skill" you would like to improve and state specific action that you will take to improve this skill. How are you going to measure and monitor your improvements?

4. Who is your mentor? Preferably someone who is 2-3 levels above you in the organization. If you are at the top of your organization, select a leadership coaching expert and / or someone with 15-20 years more experience than yours. State specific ways this person can contribute to your PDP.

Conflict Management

1. Establish agreed upon guidelines to resolving conflict (i.e. err to the side of the customer, to the highest ethical standards, to the most profitable scenario, etc.).

2. Communicate conflict management guidelines.

3. Create a culture of collaboration and relationship building within your organization by:
    • Walk around the workplace and talk to people. Ask how things are going. Ask about people's ideas and concerns.
    • Analyze your team. Are team members different in their skillset? Do they appreciate each other's differences? How do you know that?

- Define roles and responsibilities based on strengths. Explain how complementary skillsets contribute to the overall strengths of the team
- Have the team discuss, openly, how well they work together and what are the benefits of helping each other
- Ensure that each team member is heard and involve team members as much as possible in decision making, especially when the decisions are going to influence their workload, schedule, earning, rewards, and / or aspects that touches them directly

Action and Results

1. List the top 1 – 5 actions that the team should master to optimize results. What specific actions? What are the expected results? (Make sure goals are stretched but achievable).

2. Create a 1 – 5 point speech to energize people towards action. What's in it for them? What's in it for the organization? What's in it for the community at large? What are the consequences of your failure to act? What are the consequences if you did accomplish your desired outcome? Clarify the vision.

Communication

1. Clearly state your vision and / or top priorities. Let team members individually articulate their perceptions of the vision and / or priorities. Are you aligned?

2. Create an agenda for providing feedback. Jot it down on your calendar. Stick to it.

3. Examine your "active listening skills". Do you acknowledge and summarize what you hear to verify alignments especially in sensitive situations? How often do you interrupt people? How often do you use your questioning skills to bring / reveal all relevant information needed for sound decisions?

4. Ask a trusted person and / or a team-member to observe your nonverbal communication including facial expressions and body language and movements. Listen to their feedback. Or, tape yourself during a meeting and view the tape. What do you see? How can you improve?

5. Observe and review your emails and other written communication. Avoid informality whenever possible.

6. Identify a communication error that you have encountered. Analyze what went wrong. Share your findings with the team and create a solution to eliminate communication issues.

7. List the 5 toughest issues you have tackled recently and examine how effective your communication process was.

Team Building

In 1965, Bruce Wayne Tuckman hypothesized that small teams go through 4 stages: Forming, Storming, Norming, and Performing. In 1977, Tuckman, jointly with Mary Ann Jensen, added a fifth stage: Adjourning.

Early on in a teams' formation, team members get to meet each other and share information about their backgrounds, strengths, interests and experience. As team members create perceptions and impressions about each other, it is critical for the team leader to ensure that all members are involved in the formation of team norms leading to establishing clear direction regarding the task or mission at hand. This is also an opportunity for the team leader to establish his / her leadership based on professional and leadership influences not just formal authority or power.

As the team starts tackling work problems and / or moves toward achieving goals, conflicts, different opinions, clarity of roles, preferences, etc. create emotional responses. At this stage (storming) some team members may challenge the leader and / or express dissatisfaction with processes, vision, roles, etc. In this stage, it is critical for team leader to use team-building techniques to create trust, develop decision-making process, and prevent conflict.

The norming stage, characterized by developing widely accepted rules of behavior imposed by team members, are not just SOP and / or policies. Team goals become more important than individual goals. The team, however, may avoid conflict and / or tasks that potentially create conflict. The role of the leader is to ensure that potential conflict areas are discovered and tackled as well as to ensure that change, productivity, and efficiencies are gaining traction

In the "performing" stage, teams function at a very high level. Some members may never reach "star performing levels" but the team as a whole learns how to leverage every member and how to leverage all resources, so that the mission is accomplished in the most effective and efficient way. In this stage, team members trust each other and trust their leader. Diversity becomes the norm and creativity becomes a shared team talent. Leaders become less involved in decision making especially to improve the way the team work together and the way to improve results.

The "adjourning" stage can be either planned or unplanned. The planned conclusion of the teams includes recognitions and formal goodbyes. Some work teams are ongoing and the introduction of new team members may take the team back into the previously mentioned stages.

It is very important to note that teams may revert back to any stage during any given point in time. Even in the performing stage, the team may experience situations that challenge the performing norms of the team and may even result in paralyzing the team. Some of the early warning signs of team endangers include:

- New industry realities that dictate changes in skills and / or established behavioral norms of the team. (I.e. a conflict between what worked/lead to success and other factors on the horizon that will take the team into the future).
- New economic realities.
- New product and / or services needed.
- Change in the educational levels and / or training provided to team members.
- Competitions' growing market share at the expense of the team / organization.
- Technology rendering certain team's essential tools obsolete.

Leadership and Team Assimilation

The first author has personally tested and verified the following 5 step-process:

1. The leader should start by introducing himself / herself to all team members. In this step of the process, the leader should focus on all the positives that he / she observes and avoids even constructive feedback because the goal should be to "get to know each other" as humans first. In this step, the leader should ask positive exploratory, not accusatory, questions. Examples include: What is working best for you? What do you like most in this organization, assignment, etc.? Let team members share their concerns. Take notes and promise to comeback with answers. Make sure you get back with answers. Even if the leader can't provide an answer that they like or want to hear, getting back with them and explaining "why" as well as exploring alternatives is critical to success.

2. Invite the team to a leadership assimilation exercise. In this exercise, the leader should count on an independent facilitator i.e. Human Resources Professional and / or just a team-member to facilitate an exercise where the leaders leave the room allowing team members to jot down the following:
   - Things that a previous leader (or any leader) did and the team really hated.
   - Things that the team want the new leader to eliminate.
   - Their expectations of the new leader.

   The new leader should establish in this meeting his / her expectations of the team i.e. establish team "operating principles" based on the "forming stage" above.

3. Focus on few priorities and don't change direction along the way. The leader should ensure gaining team's buy-in for the selected priorities. Separate step # 2 from step # 3 by a reasonable amount of time (one month is recommended).

4. Provide weekly follow up on top selected priorities. Ask questions regarding variation of results between team members and / or different business units. Help the team overcome challenges. When performance lags carefully investigate if the barrier is a "skill" to do the job and / or "will" to get it done. Do not delay taking action, within corporate guidelines, on performance issues.

5. Create a plan for self-development and team-development based on the concepts of this book and the needs of the team / organization.

Conclusion

The concepts of leadership continue to evolve and generate lively debates as the fundamental aspects of leadership confront an ever-changing world where the interaction of cultures and advancement of technology are redefining the world, let alone leadership. In this book, we argued that while management and leadership are fundamentally situational, diversity and inclusion is vital to success in today's world. Nevertheless, there are specific principles, concepts, and requirements for effective leadership:

1. A manager can be a successful leader and vice versa. The degree to which a person spends time and efforts on aspects that are managerial in nature versus aspects that are leadership related defines the role of a person. Management has to do with command and control, planning and delegating, as well as the organization of people and processes to deliver desired results. Leadership has to do with general direction, vision, ideology, and energy to deliver the desired outcome.

2. Leadership and management can be taught; thus this book. Naturally people are born with certain skills and capabilities, but in reality successful managers and leaders emerge from all walks of life and all backgrounds. Training and development to leadership is like practice to sports' professionals.

3. Best way to measure effectiveness of leadership and management is against tangible results, improvements, and sustainability. It is important to realize that different internal and external factors, both controlled and uncontrolled, may impact results in a direct, indirect, obvious, and / or subtle ways. Regardless of results, loss of integrity is devastating to leadership and leaders.

4. Integrity is the soul of leadership, and trust is the engine of leadership

5. No one single style of management and / or leadership is good all the time for all people and / or all situations.

6. Practically, it seems futile to "box" leadership into a single dimension or a single expression. Servant leadership, ethical leadership, authentic leadership, transformational leadership, transactional leadership, charismatic leadership, collaborative leadership, autocratic leadership, democratic leadership, inspirational leadership, situational leadership, etc. are expressions that describe leaders' behaviors as they lead people and organizations. The adjectives describing the styles are self-explanatory; however, it is important to realize that leadership is about behaviors, and behaviors are usually the result of thoughts and beliefs as well as influence, power, and consequences.

7. For many businesses organizations and business leaders, diversity was a compliance issue that was managed by Human Resources professionals with some legal and moral implications. Today, diversity and inclusion has evolved to becoming a business imperative that incorporates a wide range of elements including traditional aspects such as race, gender, etc. to elements such as, sexual orientation, leadership styles, personal preferences, education, language, and diversity of talent, and contribution.

8. Diversity and inclusion plays a key role in today's organization. Emerging realities, empirical research, and ethical arguments provide a solid case for diversity. Diversity and inclusion is about empowerment of all people within an organization.

9. We propose a deep reflection process and participatory training as means to develop the inclusive leaders.

10. Change is inevitable. To manage change, organizations employ different strategies to control and guide the journey toward long-lasting and improved organizational effectiveness. Effective leaders understand the emotions of change, resistance to change, change dynamics, and use their personal flexibility to create constructive change as well as their understanding of change to guide their organizations through the cycles of change.

11. We argue that change efforts fail due to leadership failures in one way or another. Even when failure is the result of the "change design" or "change plan" it is a leadership failure.

12. The question that faces students of leadership and executives in leadership training sessions is how to

translate ideas and lessons of leadership into action and results in the workplace and / or organizations. In this book, we provide a roadmap to effective leadership that is based on the concepts of servant leadership, proper management and collaboration, change, and diversity and inclusion.

As educators and practitioners, we invite you to initiate a self-reflective journey, based on the principles of this book, to develop your roadmap to success as an effective and inclusive leader.

Dr. Amine Ayad – Rogers, Arkansas, USA. September, 2015

Dr. Emad Rahim – Syracuse, New York, USA. September, 2015

References

Academy of Management. Retrieved September 3, 2006 from: http://proquest.umi.com/pqdweb?did=769791941&Fmt=7&clientId=5728&RQT=309&VName=PQD

Aladwani, A. M., Rai, A., & Ramaprasad, A. (2000, Fall). *Database for Advances in Information Systems*, 31(4),; ABI/INFORM Global, 25.

Alleyne, S. (2005) Is Being The Best Good Enough? *Black Enterprise Magazine*. March, p. 53-54.

Andersen, M., Collins, P. (1995) *Race, Class, and Gender*. Wadsworth Publishing Company. New York, p. 101-103.

Anonymous. (2000). Overcoming the Obstacles to Leadership Development Training. *Strategies for Tomorrow*, 14(1), 20.

Anonymous. (2005). *Chain Store Age*, 81(5), 34.

Anonymous (2006) INNOVATION: Improving Your Odds. *Harvard Business Review*. Retrieved 6/10/06 from: (http://

proquest.umi.com/pqdweb?did=109755153&Fmt=7&clientId=572RQT=309&VName=PQD).

Ashforth, B., & Mael, F. (1989). Social Identity and the Organization. *Academy of Management Review*, 14(1), 20-39.

Atlanta Business Chronicle, 2003, Accidents Claim Lives of Home Depot Shoppers: http://www.bizjournals.com/atlanta/stories/2003/02/24/story2.html?page=all

August, W. S. (1997). Leadership is a Living System: Learning Leaders and Organizations. *Human Systems Management*, 16(4), 277.

Autry, James (1996). Love and Profit: Finding the Balance in Life and Work. *Quality Progress*, 29(1), 47.

Ayad, A. (2010). Business Process Improvement & Critical Thinking. *Journal of Management Development*, 29 (6), 556 – 564

Ayad, A. (2008). Optimizing Inventory and Store Results in Big Box Retail Environment. *International Journal of Retail & Distribution Management*, 36 (3), 180-191

Ayad, A. (2015). The Typology of Cyborgs and The Future of Diversity and Workplace. Retrieved from LinkedIn on 10 / 31/ 2015 from: https://www.linkedin.com/pulse/typology-cyborgs-future-diversity-workplace-amine-ayad?trk=mp-author-card

Ayad, A., Rahim, E. (2013). Leading through Diversity: Transforming Managers into Effective Leaders. Common Ground Publishing. USA

Baird-Wilkerson, S. (2003). A Monograph on Creating Organizational

Change using a Living-Systems Approach. Washington, D.C.: Institute of Education Sciences, U.S. Department of Education.

Bamford, D. R., & Forrester, P. L. (2004). Managing Planned and Emergent Change within an Operations Management Environment. *International Journal of Operations & Production Management*, 23(5), 546-564.

Barbour, R., Kitzinger, Jenny. (1999). *Developing Focus Group Research: Politics, Theory and Practice*. Los Angeles: Sage Publications.

Barnes, L. B., & Kriger, M. P. (1986). The Hidden Side of Organizational Leadership. *Sloan Management Review*, 28(1), 15.

Barone, Michael (2006). *The New Americans: How the Melting Pot Can Work Again*. New York, NY, Regnery Publishing, Inc.

Bass, B (1999). Two Decades of Research and Development in Transformational Leadership. *European Journal of Work and Organizational Psychology*, http://www.informaworld. com/smpp/title~content=t713684945~db=all ~tab=issueslist~branches=8 - v88, Issue 1 March 1999, p. 9 – 32.

Bass, B.M. (1990), *Bass & Stogdill's Handbook of Leadership: Theory, Research and Managerial Application*. New York: Simon & Schuster, Inc.

Bechtold, B. L. (1997). Chaos Theory as a Model for Strategy Development. *Empowerment in Organizations,* 5(4,), 193-201.

Becker, B. E., & Huselid, M. A. (1998). High Performance Work Systems and Firm Performance: A Synthesis of Research and Managerial Implications. *Research in Personnel and Human Resources Journal,* 16, 53–101.

Beer, M., & Nohria, N. (Eds.). (2000). *Breaking the code of change.* Boston: Harvard Business School Press.

Beeson, I., & Davis, C. (2000). Emergence and Accomplishment in Organizational Change. *Journal of Organizational Change Management,* 13(2), 178 - 189, (3rd ed.), New York: Free Press, 393-394.

Benschop, Y. (2001). Pride, prejudice and performance: relations between HRM, diversity and performance. International Journal Of Human Resource Management, 12(7), 1166-1181

Benson, R. J., Bugnitz, T. L., & Walton, W. B. (2004). *From Business Strategy to IT Action: Right Decisions for a Better Bottom Line.* Hoboken, New Jersey: Wiley.

Studi Berkun, S. (2005). *The Art of Project Management.* Sebastopol, CA: O' Reilly Media.

Bessant, J., & Haywood, B. (1985). *The Introduction of Flexible Manufacturing Systems as an Example of Computer Integrated Manufacture.* Brighton: Brighton Polytechnic.

Best, J. (2001). Telling the Truth About Damned Lies and Statistics. *The Chronicle Review*, available at: http://chronicle.com/free/v47/i34/34b00701.htm (accessed 26 December 2006).

Beverly, D., & David, R. (1999). Decision Support Software Moves HR to Center Stage. *Manufacturing Systems*, 17(10), 91.es 41 (6), p. 977–1002.

Bill, J. (1997). Make it simple!. *Strategy & Leadership*, 25(2), 34.

Black, J. A. (2000). Fermenting change: Capitalizing on the Inherent Change Found in Dynamic Non-linear (or Complex) Systems. *Journal of Organizational Change Management*, 13(6), 520-525.

Blanchard, K. H., Johnson, D. E., & Hersey, P., (2001), *Management of Organizational Behavior: Leading Human Resources*, (8th ed) Prentice-Hall, Inc., New Jersey, 124, 299.

Boje, D. M. (2000). Phenomenal Complexity Theory and Change at Disney: Response to Letiche. *Journal of Organizational Change Management*, 13(6), 558-566.

Boud D, Keogh R and Walker D (1985) *Reflection: Turning Experience in to Learning*, London: Kogan Page Publishers.

Bovee, C. L., & Thill, J. V. (2002). *Excellence in Business Communication*. Upper Saddle River, NJ: Prentice Hall.

Brady, T., & Davies, A. (2004). Building Project Capabilities: From Exploratory to Exploitative Learning. *Organization Studies*, 25(9), 1601-1621.

Brief, P., Howard, M. (1995) *Organizational Behavior: Affect in the Workplace*. Quorum Books. Connecticut, p. 41.

Brodsky, R., & Newell, E. (2007, September). The Gatekeepers. *Government Executive*, 39(16), 75-76,78-79.

Bruce, G. H., Hans, V. R., & Cary, L. C. (2002). Obstacles to Effective Organizational Change: The Underlying Reasons. *Leadership & Organization Development Journal*, 23(1/2), 6.

Browne, M.N. and Keeley, S.M. (2004), *Asking the Right Questions*, Prentice-Hall, Englewood Cliffs, NJ.

Bruce, G. H., Hans, V. R., & Cary, L. C. (2002). Obstacles to Effective Organizational Change: The Underlying Reasons. *Leadership & Organization Development Journal*, 23(1/2), 6.

Buccino, G. P. (1991). No More "Business as Usual": The Leadership Opportunity in Troubled Times. *Retail Control*, 59(5), 14.ch 6, 2009, from Alumni - ABI/INFORM Global database. (Document ID: 1347440631).

Burnes, B. (2004). *Managing Change* (4th ed.). London: Prentice-Hall.

Burns, B (2004). Kurt Lewin and the Planned Approach to Change: A Re-appraisal. *Journal of Management Studies*. 41, 977-1002.

Carnall, C. A. (1999). *Managing Change in Organization* (3rd ed.). Harlow: Prentice-Hall.

Caroselli, M (2000) *Leadership Skills for Managers.* McGraw Hill Companies Inc. USA, p. 5-28.

Chaffee, E (1985). Three Models of Strategy. *Academy of Management Review,* p. 89-98.

Chan, A. T. S., & Chan, E. H. W. (2005). Impact of Perceived Leadership Styles on Work Outcomes: Case of Building Professionals. *Journal of Construction Engineering & Management,* 131(4), 413-422.

Charan, R. (2006). Home Depot's Blueprint for Culture Change, Boston: *Harvard Business Review,* 84(4), 60–70

Charan, R., Drotter, S., & Noel, J. (2001). *The Leadership Pipeline How to Build the Leadership Powered Company,* (1st ed.), Wiley Company, Jossey- Bass, San Francisco, California, 15-30.

Chisholm, R. F. (2001). Action Research to Develop an Interorganizational Network. In P. Reason & H. Bradbury (Eds.), *Handbook of Action Research: Participative Inquiry & Practice* (pp. 324-332). London: Sage Publications, Ltd.

Choi, T. Y., Dooley, K. J., & Rungtusananatham, M. (2001). Supply Networks and Complex Adaptive Systems: Control versus Emergence. *Journal of Operations Management,* 19(3), 351-366.

Coghlan, D., & Brannick, T. (2005). *Doing Action Research in your own Organization* (2nd ed.). London: Sage Publications, Ltd.

Collins, D. (1996). New Paradigms for Change? Theories of Organization and the Organization of Theories. *Journal of Organizational Change Management,* 9(4), 9 – 23.

Cooper, C. D., Scandura, T. A., & Schriesheim, C. A. (2005). Looking Forward but Learning from our Past: Potential Challenges to Developing Authentic Leadership Theory and Authentic Leaders. *Leadership Quarterly,* 16(3), 475–493.

Clarke, M. and M. Meldrum (1999). Creating Change from Below: Early Lessons for Agents of Change. *Leadership & Organization Development Journal.* 20(2): 70.

Conger, J. A. & Nadler, D. A. N. (2004). When CEOs Step Up To Fail. *MIT Sloan Management Review,* 45(3), 50.

Coughlan, J., Lycett, M., & Macredie, R. (2003). Communication Issues in Requirements Elicitation: A Content Analysis of Stakeholder Experiences, Information, and Software Technology. *Information and Software Technology,* 45(8), 525.

Clutterbuck, David, Sheila Hirst (2002). Leadership Communication: A Status Report, *Journal of Communication Management.* London: Vol. 6, Iss. 4; pg. 351–355.

Creswell, J. W. (2003). *Research Design: Qualitative, Quantitative, and Mixed Methods Approaches.* Thousand Oaks, CA: Sage.

Crowell, C. R., & Anderson, D. C. (1982a). The Scientific and Methodological Basis of a Systematic Approach to Human Behavior Management. *Journal of Organizational Behavior Management*, 4, p. 1-32.

Culpan, R., & Trussel, J. (2005). Applying the Agency and Stakeholder Theories to the Enron Debacle: An Ethical Perspective. *Business & Society Review*, 110(1), 59-76.

Cummings, T.G. and Worley, C.G. (2001). *Organization Development and Change*, 7th ed. South-Western College Publishing: Cincinnati, OH.

Davidson, M. N., Reinemund, S., Borst, G., & Veihmeyer, J. B. (2012). How Hard Should You Push Diversity?. Harvard Business Review, 90(11), 139-143.

Davis, P., Egner, M., & Kulick, J. (2005). Implications of Modern Decision Science for Military Decision-support Systems. RAND Project Air Force, 166.

Deal, T. E. (1993). The Culture of Schools. In M. Shaskin & H. J. Walberg (Eds.), Educational Leadership and School Culture (pp. 3 – 18). Berkeley, CA: McCutchan.

Department of Defense. (1997, April 11). DoD Directive 1430.16, Defense Leadership and Management Program (DLAMP). Department of Defense. DODD, 1430.

Derek, N. (1998). Vendors aren't Keeping Pace with User Demand. *Computing Canada*, 24(23), 31.

Derek, R. A., Scott, T., Kristin, H. G., & Miguel, A. Q. (2003). The Impact Measures of Leader Experience on Leader Effectiveness: New insights for Leader Selection. *Journal of Business Research*, 56(8), 673.

Dickman, N. (2005). Definition of market research: What is qualitative research? Retrieved December 11, 2007, from Market Research World Web site:http://www.marke tresearchworld.net/index.php?option=com content& task=view&id=11&Itemid=64

Diefenbach, T. (2007). The Managerialistic Ideology of Organisational Change Management. *Journal of Organizational Change Management*, 20(1), 126-144.

DiMaggio, P. (1995). Comments on "What theory is not." *Administrative Science Quarterly*, 40(3), 391-397.

DoD Instruction 1100.22. (2006, September 7). Guidance for Determining Workforce Mix.

DoD 5200.1-R. (1982, August). Information Security Program Regulation.

DoD Instruction 5000.2. (2003, May 12). Operation of the Defense Acquisition System.

DoD Directive 5000.01. (2003, May 12). The Defense Acquisition System.

DoD Directive 5200.28. (1978, April). [Revised.]. Security Requirements for Automatic Data Processing (ADP) Systems.

DoD Directive 8000.01. (2002, February 27). Management of DoD Information *Resources and Information Technology.*

Donald, E. G., & Scott, J. S. (2003). Who Ought to be Blamed? The Effect of Organizational Roles on Blame and Credit Attributions. *International Journal of Conflict Management*, 14(2), 95.

Donnelly, J. H. J. (1994). Reframing the mind of the banker: The changing skill set and skill mix for effective leadership. *The International Journal of Bank Marketing* 12(8): 12.

Douglas, A. R. (2004). How to Grow Great Leaders. *Harvard Business Review*, 82(12), 92.

Drucker, P. F. (1987). The Knowledge Economy. In A. E. Cawkell (Ed.), *Evolution of an Information Society* (pp.76-92). Aslib: London.

Durand, R., & Colari, R. (2006). Sameness, Otherness? Enriching Organizational Change Theories with Philosophical Considerations on the Same and the Other. *Academy of Management Review* 31(1), 93-113.

Facione, P.A. (1990), Executive Summary – Critical Thinking. A Statement of Expert Consensus for Purposes of Educational Assessment and Instruction, California Academic Press, Millbrae, CA.

Farson, R,. Keyes, R. F., (2002). The Failure-Tolerant Leader. *Harvard Business Review*, 80(8), 64.

Feldman, D.C. (2004). What are We Talking about When We Talk about Theory? *Journal of Management*, 30(5), 565-567.

Ferrarie, K. E. (2005). Processes to Assess Leadership Potential Keeps Shell's Talent Pipeline Full. *Journal of Organizational Excellence*, 24(3), 17.

Fichter, D. (2003). Why Web Projects Fail. [Electronic version]. *New Zealand Management*, 27(4). Retrieved January 20, 2008, from Business Source Premier Database at http://www.ebscohost.com

Flood, R. L. (2001). The Relationship of 'Systems Thinking' to Action Research. In P. Reason & H. Bradbury (Eds.), *Handbook of Action Research: Participative Inquiry & Practice* (pp. 133-144). London: SAGE Publications, Ltd.

Follett, M.P. (1924), *Creative Experience*, Peter Smith, New York, NY. Pg. 19

Follett, M.P. (1940d), Power, in Metcalf, H.C. and Urwick, L. (Eds), *Dynamic Administration: The Collected Papers of Mary Parker Follett.* Harper & Brothers Publishers, New York, NY, pp. 95-116.

Follett, M.P. (1940e), The Meaning of Responsibility in Business Management, in Metcalf, H.C. and Urwick, L. (Eds), *Dynamic Administration: The Collected Papers of Mary Parker Follett.* Harper & Brothers Publishers, New York, NY, pp. 146-66.

Ford, M. W., & Greer, B. M. (2006). Profiling Change: An Empirical Study of Change Process Patterns. *The Journal of Applied Behavioral Science*, 42(4), 420–446.

Fowke, D., Shepard, PhD, K., Koplowitz, PhD, H., & Dutrisac, M., (2005), The New Management Network, *Toronto*, Vol. 15, (1) pg 1.

Frances, H. (2005). Seeing Things Whole. *Leader to Leader*, 2005(37), 4.

Franzoi, Stephen. (1996). *Social Psychology*. Chicago: Brown and Benchmark Publishing.

French, W. L., Bell, Jr., C. H., et al. (2000). *Organization Development and Transformation: Managing Effective Change*. New York: McGraw-Hill.

Friedman, Thomas (2007). *The World is Flat*. New York, NY: Farrar, Straus, and Giroux.

Gadiesh, O., Gilbert, J (2000) Transforming Corner-Office / Strategy into Frontline Action. *Harvard Business Review on Advances in Strategy*. Harvard Business School Press.

Galbraith, J., Downey, D. and Kates, A. (2002). *Designing Dynamic Organizations*. New York: AMACOM.

Gibson, Ivancevich, Donnelly, & Konopaske (2003). *Organizations: Behavior, Structure, Processes*, 11th Edition. Boston: McGraw Hill.

Gilbert, D. (2002). *The American Class Structure: In an Age of Growing Inequality.*

Belmont, CA: Wadsworth; Thompson, W. & Hickey, J. (2005).

Gilbert, E. and B. H. Kleiner (1993). Learning to love change. *Leadership & Organization Development Journal* 14(5): I.

Gilchrist, A. (2000). The Well-connected Community: Networking to the Edge of Chaos. *Community Development Journal*, 3(3), 264-275.

Gill, R. (2003) Change Management or Change Leadership? *Journal of Change Management* 3(4): 307.

Gharajedaghi, J. (2006). *Systems Thinking: Managing Chaos and Complexity: A Platform for Designing Business Architecture*. Burlington, MA: Elsevier.

Ghoshal, S. and Bartlett, C. (1997), From Organization Man to the Individualized Corporation, presented at the 1997 Strategic Management Society Conference, October.

Greenfield, T. B. (1973). Organizations as Social Inventions: Rethinking Assumptions about Change. *Journal of Applied Behavioral Science*, 9(5), 551-573.

Greenleaf, R. K. (2002). *Servant Leadership: A Journey into the Nature of Legitimate Power and Greatness*. Paulist Press. New York/Mahwah, N.J.

Greenwood, R., & Hinings, C. R. (1993). Understanding Strategic Change: The Contribution of Archetypes. *Academy of Management Journal*, 36(5), 1052 – 1081.

Greenwood, Davydd, and Levin, Morten (2007). *Introduction to Action Research*. Thousand Oaks, CA: 2007.

Groves, K. S. (2005). Linking Leader Skills, Follower Attitudes, and Contextual Variables via an Integrated Model of Charismatic Leadership. *Journal of Management*, 31(2), 255-277.

Gulick, L., & Urwick L., (1937). *Papers on the Science of Administration*. New York: Institute of Public Administration, 3-13.

Hagberg, R. (1996). Identify and help executives in trouble. *HR Magazine*, 41(8), 88.

Hahn, B (2006) The MBA is Far From Dead. *Rutland Herald*. Retrieved July 5, 2006 from: (http://www.rutlandherald.com/apps/pbcs.dll/article?AID=/20040906/NES409060303/1011/BUSINESS).

Hamilton, N. (2005). Ex-Morgan Stanley Execs use Edelman to oust CEO. *PR Week*, 8(17), 2.

Hardgrave, B., & Armstrong, D. (2005, November). Software Process Improvement: It's a Journey, Not a Destination. *Communications of the ACM*, 48(11).

Harris, S. (2004, August). Mr. Fixit. *Government Executive*, 36(14), 84-88. Retrieved March 6, 2009, from Alumni – ABI/INFORM Global database. (Document ID: 684909391).

Harry, G. (2005). Strategy and Leadership. *Development and Learning in Organizations*, 19(1), 5.

Hatch, M (1997) *Organization Theory*. Oxford University Press. UK.

Heifetz, M. and S. Halle (1996) Leading change, overcoming chaos--making change succeed in your organization. *Hospital Materiel Management Quarterly* 18(1): 17.

Hellriegel, D., Slocum, J., & Woodman, R., (2001), *Organizational Behaviors*. South-Western College Publishing, (9th ed.), Mason, pg. 4-5

Herzig, S. E., & Jimmieson, N. L. (2006). Middle Managers' Uncertainty Management during Organizational Change. *Leadership & Organization Development Journal* 27(8), 628 - 645.

Hiatt, J., & Creasey, T. C. (2005). *Change Management: The People Side of Change*. Loveland, CO: Prosci Research.

Hofstede, G. (2001). *Culture's Consequences, Comparing Values, Behaviors, Institutions, and Organizations Across Nations*. Thousands Oaks, CA: Sage Publications, Inc.

Hollander, E., Offermann, L (1990) Power and Leadership in Organizations. *American Psychologist*, Vol. 45, No. 2, p. 179-189

Holley, Jr.,W., Jennings, K. M. et al. (2005). *The Labor Relations Process*. Mason, OH: Thomson South-Western.

Horton, T., (2000). Teaming up with the Team. *Directors and Boards*, 25(1), 10.

Houchin, K., & MacLean, D. (2005). Complexity Theory and Strategic Change: An Empirically Informed Critique. *British Journal of Management*, 16(2), 149-166.

Howell, J. M., & Avolio, B. J. (1992). The Ethics of Charismatic Leadership: Submission or Liberation? *Academy of Management Executive*, 6,43−54.

Hunter, J., (2004) *The World's Most Powerful Leadership Principles: How to Become a Servant Leader.*, New York, Crown Business, (9th ed.), 99.

Hurley, R. F. (2006). The Decision to Trust. *Harvard Business Review* 84(9): 55-62.

Ingram, L. (1995) *The Study of Organizations: Position, Persons and Patterns.* Praeger. Connecticut, p. 58-61.

IT Governance Institute (2003). Board Briefing on IT Governance (2nd ed.) Retrieved May 11, 2008, from http://www.isaca.org/Content/ ContentGroups/ITGI3/Resources1/Board_Briefing_ on_IT_Governance/26904_Board_Briefing_final.pdf

James, R. S. (2003). Where's the leader? *The RMA Journal*, 86(4), 36.

Jaques, E. (1997). *Requisite Organization: Total System for Effective Managerial Organization and Managerial Leadership for the 21st Century.* London: Gower.

Jarvis, P., (1999). *The Practitioner-Researcher.* San Francisco. Jossey-Bass. 129, 131, 52, 172.

Jaskyte, K., Kisieliene, A. (2006) Organizational innovation: A comparison of nonprofit human-service organizations in Lithuania and the United States. *International Social Work*. Retrieved 6/24/06 from: (http://proquest.umi. com/pqdweb?did=1034753141&Fmt=7&clientId=572 &RQT=309&VName=PQD).

Jimba, S. W. (1998). Information Technology, Globalization and Africa's Information Development. *OCLC systems and services*, 14(2), 64-70.

John, B. W., & Christine, C. (1999). The Two Faces of Leadership. *Career Development International*, 4(3), 146.

John, R. B. (2004). The Value of Failure. *Industry Week*, 253(4), 23.

John, Q. (1999). DSS Software can Help Predict Effects of Changes. *Computing Canada* 25(24), 31.

John, W. S., Jr., Cass, R., & Albert, C. (2002). On Death and Dying: The Corporate Leadership Capacity of CEOs. *Organizational Dynamics*, 30(3), 269.

Johnson, James A (1998) Interview with Warren Bennis, Chairman, *The Leadership Institute Journal of Healthcare Management*. Chicago: Jul/Aug. Vol.43, Issue. 4; pg. 293-297.

Johnson, M. (2004) *Working While Black*. Lawrence Hill Books. Illinois, p. 49-82.

Jones, G. (2007). *Organizational Theory, Design, and Change* (5th ed.). Upper Saddle River, New Jersey: Prentice Hall.

Jones, M., Cline, M., & Ryan, S. (2006, January). Exploring Knowledge Sharing in ERP Implementation: An Organizational Culture Framework. *Decision Support Systems*, 41(2), 411.

Kanungo, R. N. (2001). Ethical Values of Transactional and Transformational Leaders. *Canadian Journal of Administrative Sciences*, 18,257−265.

Kanter, R. M. (1997). *World class: Thriving Locally in the Global Economy.* New York: Simon and Schuster.

Kanter, R. M., Stein, B. A., & Jick, T. D. (1992). The Challenge of Organizational Change. New York: Free Press.

Kearney, A. T. (1989). *Computer Integrated Manufacturing: Competitive Advantage or Technological Dead End?* London: A.T. Kearney.

Kent, R. (2001) *Installing Change: An Executive Guide for Implementing and Maintaining Organizational Change.* Winnipeg: Pragma Press, Inc.,

Kotter, J. (1996). *Leading Change.* MA: Harvard Business School Press.

Kreitner, R., Kinicki, A. (2003) *Organizational Behavior,* Sixth Edition. The McGraw-Hill Companies. p. 559-684.

Kerzner, H. (2003). *Project Management: A Systems Approach to Planning, Scheduling, and Controlling* (8th ed.). Hoboken, NJ: Wiley.

Konstantinos, A. (2006). Design and Implementation of a Decision Support System for Assigning Human Resources in the Hellenic Navy. Monterey, CA: Naval Postgraduate School.

Kuzela, L. (1984). Intrapreneurs Help Big Firms 'Think Small'. *Industry Week, 222*(4), 39.

Larraine, S. (1998). Strategic Alliances for the 21st century. *Strategy & Leadership, 26*(4), 12.

Lester, R. I. (2004). AU-24 Concepts for Air Force Leadership. Retrieved March 12, 2007, 2007, from http://www.au.af.mil/au/awc/awcgate/au-24/contents.htm

Lofland, J., Snow, D., Anderson, L., & Lofland, L. (2006). Analyzing Social Settings: A Guide to Qualitative Observation and Analysis. Belmont, CA: Wadsworth/Thompson Learning.

Lewin, K. (1947). Frontiers in group dynamics. In D. Cartwright (Ed.), *Field Theory in Social Science*. London: Social Science Paperbacks.

Lewin, K. (1951). *Field Theory in Social Science: Selected Theoretical Papers* (D. Cartwright, Ed.). New York: Harper & Brothers.

Lewis, R. (1994). From Chaos to Complexity: Implications for Organizations. *Executive Development, 7*(4), 16-17.

Liu, W., Lepak, D., Takeuchi, R., & Sims, H. (2003). Matching Leadership Styles with Employment Modes:

Strategic Human Resource Perspective. *Human Resource Management Review*, 13, 127-152.

Lloyd, M. and S. Maguire (2002). The possibility horizon. *Journal of Change Management* 3(2): 149.

Lum, D. (1999). *Culturally Competent Practice*. Brooks/Cole Publishing Company. New York. p. 19-42.

Lumpkin, G. T., & Lichtenstein, B. B. (2005). The Role of Organizational Learning in the Opportunity-Recognition Process. *Entrepreneurship: Theory & Practice*, 29(4), 451-472.

Macbeth, D. K. (2002). Emergent Strategy in Managing Cooperative Supply Chain Change. *International Journal of Operations and Production Management*, 22(7), 728-740.

Maccoby, M., Gittell, H., J., Ledeen, M. (2004). Leadership and the Fear Factor. *MIT Sloan Management Review*, 45(2), 14.

MacD Marcus, M. (1983). Power Politics and MIS Implementation. *Association for Computing Technology*, 26(6), 430-444.

Maggie, B. (1999). Decision-Support Products Track Leading Performance Metrics, Application Usage. InfoWorld, 21(32), 54.

Manning, T. (2002). Strategic conversation as a tool for change. *Strategy & Leadership* 30(5): 35.

Mark Rittacco a Burke, W. W., & Litwin, G. H. (1992). A Causal Model of Organizational Performance and Change. *Journal of Management*, 18, 523-545.

Marshak, R. J. (1993). Lewin meets Confucius: A Review of the OD Model of Change. *The Journal of Applied Behavioral Science*, 29(4), 393-415.

Marshall, G. (1998). Qualitative versus Quantitative Debate. Retrieved December 11, 2007, from High Beam Encyclopedia Web site: http://www.encyclopedia.com/doc/1O88-qualitativeverssqntttvdbt.html

Mary Ann Von, G. (2005). The CCL Guide to Leadership in Action: How Managers and Organizations Can Improve the Practice of Leadership. *The Academy of Management Review*, 30(2), 440.

Mary, W. C., & Donald, C. A. (2002). Failure: Lessons for Health Care Leaders. *Nursing Economics*, 20(5), 225.

Marx, K., & Engels, F. (1848), The Communist Manifesto. Retrieved October 5, 2007, from MIA Web site: http://www.marxists.org/archive/marx/works/1848/communist-manifesto/index.htm

Mastenbroek, W. F. G. (1996). Organizational Innovation in Historical Perspective: Change as Duality Management. *Business Horizons* (39), 5-14.

Mastenbroek, W. F. G. (2004). *Organizational Innovation in Historical Perspective: Change as Duality Management.* Farmington Hills, MI: Gale Group.

Matheson, I. and Matheson, J. (1998), The Smart Organization. *Harvard Business School Press*, Boston, MA.

May, G. L. (2005). Incorporating a Career Planning Lab into a Managerial Communications Course. *Business Communication Quarterly*, 68(3), 345-357.

Maxwell, J. A. (2005). *Qualitative Research Design: An Interactive Approach* (Vol. 41). Thousand Oaks: Sage Publications, Inc.

McAdams, T., Neslund, N., et al. (2004). *Law, Business, & Society*. New York, NY: McGraw-Hill.

McCain, J. W., & Hudson, S. K. (2003). *Technology, Transfer and Commercialization*. Athens, AL: Design Unlimited.

McGrath, J. E., Arrow, H., & Berdahl, J.L. (2000). The Study of Groups: Past, Present, and Future. *Personality & Social Psychology Review*, 4(1), 95-106.

McNish, M. (2002). Guidelines for Managing Change: A Study of their Effects on the Implementation of New Information Technology Projects in Organizations." *Journal of Change Management* 2(3): 201.

Miner, J.B. (2003). The Rated Importance, Scientific Validity, and Practical Usefulness of Organizational Behavior Theories: A Quantitative Review. *Academy of Management Learning and Education*, 2(3), 250-258.

Michael, G. (2004). Former State Department Official Speaks in Des Moines. *The Washington Report on Middle East Affairs*, 23(8), 79.

Michie, S., & Gooty, J. (2005). Values, Emotions, and Authenticity: Will the Real Leader Please Stand Up? *Leadership Quarterly*, 16(3), 441-457.

Miller, D., & Freisen, P. H. (1984). *Organizations: A Quantum View*. Englewood Cliffs: Prentice-Hall, Inc.

Miller, C. C., & Ireland, R. D. (2005). Intuition in Strategic Decision Making: Friend or Foe in the Fast-Paced 21century?, *Academy of Management Executive*, 19(1), 19-30.

Mintzberg, H. (1996) Managing Government, Governing Management. *Harvard Business Review* 74:3, pp. 75-83.

Mintzberg, H., Waters, A (1982). Tracking Strategy in Entrepreneurial Firms, *Academy of Management*, Vol. 25, 3, p. 465-499.

Mitchell, T. R. (1973). Motivation and Participation: An Integration. *Academy of Management Journal*, 16(4), 670-679.

Mitchell, T. R., & Scott, W. G. (1987). Leadership Failures, the Distrusting Public, and Prospects of the Administrative State. *Public Administration Review*, 47(6), 445.

Montuori, L. A. (2000). Organizational Longevity: Integrating Systems Thinking, Learning and Conceptual Complexity. *Journal of Organizational Change Management* 13(1): 61.

Moore, M. H. (1995) *Creating Public Value: Strategic Management in Government*. Harvard University Press, Cambridge, MA.

Moran, J., & Avergun, A. (1997). Creating Lasting Change. *The TQM Magazine* 9(2), 146 - 151.

Moran, J. W. and B. K. Brightman (2001). Leading organizational change. *Career Development International* 6(2/3): 111.

Muczyk, J. P., & Reimann, B. C. (1987). The Case for Directive Leadership. *The Academy of Management Executive*, 1(4), 301.

Mullins, L. J. (2002). *Management and Organizational Behavior* (6th ed.). Harlow: Prentice-Hall.

Myers, D., & Banerjee, T. (2005). Toward Greater Heights for Planning. *Journal of the American Planning Association*, 71(2), 121-129.

Nadler, D., & Tushman, M. (1980). A Model for Diagnosing Organizational Behavior. *Organizational Dynamics*, 9(2), 35-51.

Nadler, D. A., Shaw, R. B., & Walton, A. E. (1995). *Discontinuous Change: Leading Organizational Transformation*. San Francisco: Jossey-Bass.

Nancy, Z. D. (1998). Leadership in Quality Organizations. *The Journal for Quality and Participation*, 21(1), 32.

New, C. (1989). The Challenge of Transformation. In B. Burnes & B. Weeks (Eds.), *AMT: A Strategy for Success?* London: NEDO.

North Carolina Department of Environment and Natural Business. (1999). Rapid Application Development Method. Retrieved December 17, 2006, from Information Technology Services Division Web site: http://www.enr.state.nc.us/its/pdf/Section6-rad.pdf

Northouse, P. (2007). *Leadership Theory and Practice.* Thousand Oaks, CA: Sage Publications.

Obama, Barack (2008). *The Audacity of Hope: Thoughts on Reclaiming the American Dream.* New York, NY: Vintage.

O'Donovan, J. (2006). *The Corporate Culture Handbook: How to Plan, Implement, and Measure a Successful.* Ireland: Liffey Press, Ashbrook House.

Owen, C. (2005). Command Failure in War: Psychology and Leadership. *The American Historical Review,* 110(3), 766.

Palmer, K. (2005, September). Now Hiring. *Government Executive,* 37(16), 65-82. Retrieved March 6, 2009, from Alumni - ABI/INFORM Global database. (Document ID: 904912971).

Peters, T. (1997). *The Circle of Innovation: You can't Shrink your Way to Greatness.* New York: Alfred A. Knopf.

PMI. (2004). *A Guide to the Project Management Body of Knowledge.* Newton Square, PA: Project Management Institute.

PMI. (2005). Project Management: Process areas. Retrieved December 1, 2006, from www.pmi.org

MI Standards Committee. (2006). *The Standard for Program Management*. Newton Square, PA: Project Management Institute.

Pollard, C. W. (2006). *Serving Two Masters? Reflections on God and Profit*. HarperCollins Publishers. New York, New York.

Prasad, P. (2005). *Crafting Qualitative Research*. Armonk, New York: M. E. Sharpe.

Purdue, D. (2001). Neighborhood Governance: Leadership Trust and Social Capital. *Urban Studies: Reclaiming Children and Youth*. Volume 38, No. 12, 2211-2224.

Purser, R. E., & Petranker, J. (2005). Unfreezing the Future: Exploring the Dynamic of Time in Organizational Change. *The Journal of Applied Behavioral Science*, 41(2), 182-203.

Rahim, E., & Dawson, M. (2010). Emerging Trends: IT project Management in a Global Market. *Journal of Information Systems Technology and Planning.*

Reynolds, K. T. (2003). *An IT and Security Comparison Decision Support System for Wireless LANs*. Boca Raton, FL: Universal Publishers/uPUBLISH.com.

Ridge, R. A. (2005). A Dynamic Duo: Staff Development and You. *Nursing Management*, 36(7), 28-35.

Robbins, S. (2003) *Organizational Behavior*. Prentice Hall. New Jersey, p. 3-58.

Robert, F. R. (2004). When Leadership Fails. *Strategic Finance*, 86(6), 19.

Robert, L. Z. (2000). Teaching Agricultural Ethics. *Journal of Agricultural and Environmental Ethics*, 13(3-4), 229.

Robert, F. R. (2004). When Leadership Fails. *Strategic Finance*, p. 78-88.

Reason, P., & Bradbury, H. (2001). *Handbook of Action Research*. Thousand Oaks, CA: Sage.

Robbins, S. P. (2005). *Organizational Behavior.* Upper Saddle River, NJ: Prentice Hall.

Roberts, Jr., T., Gibson, M., Fields, K., & Rainer, Jr., R. (1998). *Factors that Impact Implementing.* IEEE Transactions on Software Engineering, 24(8), 640-649.

Rubin, H., & Rubin, I. (2005). *Qualitative Interviewing: The Art of Hearing Data.* Thousand Oaks: Sage.

Ryan, David. (2000). *US Foreign Policy in World History.* London: Rutledge Publishing.

Sandi, M. (2003). Why CEOs Fail: The 11 Behaviors That Can Derail Your Climb to the Top. *Leadership & Organization Development Journal*, 24(7/8), 473.

Sastry, M. A. (1997). Problems and Paradoxes in a Model of Punctuated Organizational Change. *Administrative Science Quarterly*, 42, 237-275.

Schein, E. H. (1968). Personal Change Through Interpersonal Relationships. In Bennis, W. G., Schein, E. H., Steele, F. 1. & Berlew, D. E. (Eds.) *Interpersonal Dynamics*. Rev. Ed. Homewood, 111.: Dosey Press.

Schein, E. H. (1992) *Organizational Culture and Leadership*. 2d. Ed. San Francisco, CA.: Jossey Bass.

Scholey, C. (2005). Strategy Maps: A Step-by-Step Guide to Measuring, Managing and Communicating the Plan. *Journal of Business Strategy*, 26(3), 12-19.

Schon D (1991) *The Reflective Practitioner How Professionals Think in Action*, London: Avebury.

Schwandt, D. R. (2005). When Managers Become Philosophers: Integrating Learning With Sensemaking. *Academy of Management Learning & Education*, 4(2), 176-192.

Shafritz, J., Ott, J., & Yong Suk, J. (2005). *Classics of Organizational Theory* (6th ed.). Belmont, California: Thomson/Wadsworth.

Shelton, C. K., & Darling, J. R. (2001). The Quantum Skills Model in Management: A New Paradigm to Enhance Effective Leadership. *Leadership and Organization Development Journal*, 22(6), 264-273.

Selznick, P., (1957). *Leadership in Administration: A Sociological Interpretation*. Harper & Rowe Publishers, New York, 100.

Senge, P. M., (1996). The Ecology of Leadership. *Leader to Leader*, 2 Fall, http://leadertoleader.org/leaderbooks/ L2L/fall96/senge.html, 18-23.

Silverman, L., Taliento, L (2006). What Business Execs Don't Know, But Should About Nonprofits. *Stanford Social Innovation Review*. Stanford University. Retrieved 11/16/2006 from: http://www.ssireview.org/search/results/63c30d74da934f0ee5cf4fc53a66ad13/

Simonaitiene, B., Leonaviciene, R., Zvirdauskas, D. (2004). Manifestation of Leader's Communicative and Educational Abilities as a Premise for Learning Organization Development. *Socialiniai Mokslai*. Nr.4 (46). Kaunus University of Technology.

Slater, R. (2002). *Jack Welch & The G.E. Way: Management Insights and Leadership Secrets of the Legendary CEO*. New York, N.Y.: McGraw-Hill.

Smeltzer, J (2004) Driving Performance through Knowledge Management. *Consulting's Behavioral Services Group*. 28(1), p. 15.

Simon, S., Varun, G., Teng, J., & Kathleen, W. (1996). Training Methods and Cognitive Ability to End-user Satisfaction, Comprehension, and Skill Transfer: A Longitudinal Field Study. *Information Systems Research*, 7(4), 466-490.

Spreitzer, G.M. (1995). Psychological Empowerment in the Workplace: Dimensions, Measurement, and Validation. *Academy of Management Journal*, 38, 1442–1465.

Skills, S. C. (2004). Events & News: The Partnership for 21st Century Skills Web. Retrieved March 15, 2007, from http://www.21stcenturyskills.org/index.php?option=com_content&task=view&id=250&Itemid=64

Sonnenfeld, J. A. (1985). Shedding Light on the Hawthorne Studies. *Journal of Occupational Behavior*, 6(2), 110-130.

Sprague, R.H. (1980). A Framework for the Development of Decision Support Systems. *MIS Quarterly*, 4, 1-26.

Srinivasan, M. (2005). Knowledge Management for Software Companies. The Project Perfect White Paper Collection. Retrieved April 5, 2009, from http://www.projectperfect.com.au/downloads/Info/ info_knowledge_management.pdf

Stace, D., & Dunphy, D. (2001). *Beyond the Boundaries: Leading and Recreating the Successful Enterprise* (2nd ed.). Sydney, Australia: McGraw-Hill.

Stacey, R. D., Griffin, D., & Shaw, P. (2002). *Complexity and Management: Fad or Radical Challenge to Systems Thinking.* London: Routledge.

Stephen, R. M. (2005). Best-in-Class Leadership. *Leadership Excellence*, 22(3), 17.

Stevens, J. A. (2003, August). *The Motivations-Attributes-Skills-Knowledge Competency Cluster Validation Model: An Empirical Study.* Doctoral dissertation, Texas A&M University. Available electronically from http : / / handle .tamu .edu /1969 .1 /339

Stockdale, Margaret, Crosby, Faye (2003). *The Psychology and Management of Workplace Diversity.* London: Wiley-Blackwell.

Strassmann, P. (1997). The Squandered Computer Published. *Cutter IT Journal*. New Canaan, CT: The Information Economics Press.

Stringer, Ernest (2007). *Action Research*. London: Sage Publications.

Subeliani, D., & Tsogas, G. (2005). Managing diversity in the Netherlands: a case study of Rabobank. International Journal Of Human Resource Management, 16(5), 831-851.

Sujansky, J. G. (2004). Seven Mistakes Leaders Make. *Restaurant Hospitality*, 88(6), 12.

Sutton, R., & Straw, B., (1995). What Theory is Not. *Administrative Science Quarterly*, 40(3), 371-384.

Stahl, R. A. and S. L. Andersen (1996) Leadership and Change Management. *Hospital Materiel Management Quarterly* 17(3): 54.

Sydney, F. (2004). Why Smart Executives Fail. *Executive Excellence*, p. 12-35.

Thatchenkery, Tojo, and Metzker, Carol. (2006). *Appreciative Intelligence: Seeing the Mighty Oak in the Acorn*. San Francisco, CA: Berrett-Koehler Publishers, Inc.

Tesch, R. (1990). *Qualitative Research: Analysis Types and Software Tools*. New York: The Falmer Press.

Tetenbaum, T. (1998). Shifting Paradigms from Newton to Chaos. *Organizational Dynamics*, 26(4), 21-32.

The Syracuse Post-Standard, News Service Report, Census Bureau (2005) Newspaper. March 29 article. 6 (B).

Thomas, Roosevelt. (1991). *Beyond Race and Gender Unleashing the Power of Your Total Work Force by Managing Diversity.* New York, NY: AMACOM.

Tichy, N. (1983). The Essentials of Strategic Change Management. *Journal of Business Strategy,* 3(4), 55-67.

Trudell, L. (2002). Thriving on Organizational Change: The Knowledge Sharing Advantage. Retrieved from: http://quantum.dialog.com/q2_resources/whitepapers/thriving.pdf

Tsui, A., Zhang, Z., Wang, H., Xin, K., Wu, J. (2006) Unpacking the Relationship between CEO Leadership Behavior and Organizational Culture. *Leadership Quarterly.* Retrieved 6/10/06 from: (http://proquest.umi.com/pqdweb?did=1062975581&Fmt=7&clientId=5728&RQT=309&VName=PQD).

Tuckman, B. W. (1965). Developmental Sequence in Small Groups. *Psychological Bulletin,* 63(6), 384-399.

Tuckman, Bruce W., and Mary-Ann C. Jensen (1977). Stages of Small-group Development Revisited. *Group & Organization Studies,* vol. 2 (no. 4):419-427.

Tzu, Sun (Circa 550BC) *The Art of War.* China.

Turban, E., & Rainer, Jr., R. K., et al. (2003). *Introduction to Information Technology.* Hoboken, NJ: Wiley.

Turcotte, W. E. (2004). Executive Strategy Issues for Very Large Organizations. *AU-24 Concepts for Air Force Leadership* (4th ed.). Retrieved March 24, 2007, from http://www.au.af.mil/au/awc/awcgate/au-24/contents.htm

Turcotte, W. E. (2001, August). Executive Strategy Issues for Very Large Organizations. Air Force Officer Training Manual, Air University: Maxwell AFB, AL.

Tyson, S. (1992). Business and Human Resource Strategy. *Irish Business and Administrative Research* (13), 1-5.

University of Arkansas for Medical Science Cultural Sensitivity Test. Retrieved September 5, 2015 from: http://www.uams.edu/diversity/test.asp

USA TODAY. Retrieved July 5, 2006 from: (http://www.usatoday.com/news/education/2005-04-19-mba-usat_x.htm)

US Department of Defense (2002). http://www.defenselink.mil/pubs/dod101/dod_101_for_2002.html. Accessed April 7, 2007. DOD 101: An Introductory Overview of the Department of Defense.

US Office of Personnel Management (September 2006) US Federal Government Human Capital Survey.

Vaughn, S., Schumm, J. S., & Sinagub, J. (1996). *Focus Group Interviews in Education and Psychology.* Thousand Oaks, CA: Sage.

Vogl, A. J. (2003). Understanding Failure. *Across the Board*, 40(4), 27.

Walls, H (2003). Managing to Lead. *Industrial Engineer*, 35(5), 22.

Wal-Mart (2007). http://www.walmartfacts.com. Accessed April 7, 2008.

Wang, E., Chen, H., Jiang, J., & Klein, G. (2005). Interaction Quality between IS Professionals and Users: Impacting Conflict and Project Performance. *Journal of Information Science*, 31(4), 273.

Watson, A., & Wooldridge, B. (2005). Business Unit Manager Influence on Corporate-level Strategy Formulation. *Journal of Managerial Issues*, 17(2), 147-161.

Weber, Max (1947) *The Theory of Social and Economic Organization*. Translated by A. M. Henderson & Talcott Parsons, The Free Press.

Weber, R. Camerer, C., Rottensteich, Y., & Knez, M. (2001). The Illusion of Leadership: Misattribution of Cause in Coordination Games. *Organization Science*, 12(5), 582.

Weick, K. E. (1995). What Theory is Not, Theorizing is. *Administrative Science Quarterly*, 40(3), 385-390.

Wendel, F. C., Hoke, F. A., & Joekel, R. G. (1996). Outstanding School Administrators: Their Keys to Success // Review. *Canadian Journal of Education*, 21(3), 333.

Weymes, E. (2003) Relationships not Leadership Sustain Successful Organizations. *Journal of Change Management* 3(4): 319.

Wheatley, M. J. (1999). *Leadership and the New Science* (2nd ed.). San Francisco: Barrett-Koehler.

Whetten, D. A. (2001). What Constitutes a Theoretical Contribution? *Academy of Management Review*, 14(4), 490-495.

Wirtenberg, J., Abrams, L., & Ott, C. (2004). Assessing the Field of Organization Development. *The Journal Of Applied Behavioral Science*, 40(4), 465-479.

Worley, C., Hitchin, D. and Ross, W. (1996). *Integrated Strategic Change: How OD Builds Competitive Advantage.* MA: Addison-Wesley Publishing.

Wuthnow, Robert (2007). *America and the Challenges of Religious Diversity.* Princeton, NJ: Princeton University Press.

Xavier, S. (2005). Are you at the top of your game? Checklist for Effective Leaders. *Journal of Business Strategy*, 26(3), 35-42.

Yukl, G. (2001). *Leadership in Organizations.* Jersey City, NJ: Prentice Hall.

Yukl, G. (2002). *Leadership in Organizations.* Prentice Hall. New Jersey, p. 273-275.

Dr. Ayad is a Scholar-Practitioner and accomplished business leader with over twenty-five years of experience in leading multi-billion businesses, developing and implementing strategies, designing and sustaining effective processes, and engaging employees at all levels leading to improved top line and bottom line business results.

As an adjunct professor, Dr. Ayad has taught at Strayer University in Columbus, Ohio, Centennial College in Ontario, Canada, Bellevue University in Omaha, Nebraska, and Colorado Technical University, in Colorado Springs, Colorado. He has authored and coauthored several papers on business and management topics in journals such as International Journal of Retail and Distribution Management, Journal of Management, International Journal of Project Organization and Management, and Quality Progress.

Dr. Ayad has worked for Home Depot, Sears Holdings, and Walmart where he served as a District Manager, Divisional Director of Merchandising, and Senior Director of Strategy and Innovation. Currently, he serves in a leadership role at Bed Bath and Beyond. During his journey, Dr. Ayad witnessed the advantages and disadvantages as well as the successes and disappointments of transformation through teaching case studies for his MBA and doctorate students as well as through his action-based research and reflective approach.

Dr. Ayad graduated with honors from Oklahoma State University as a Civil Engineer. He holds a Doctorate in Management degree from Colorado Technical University.

Dr. Emad Rahim is an award-winning Author, Educator, Entrepreneur, Fulbright Scholar and TEDx Speaker. Dr. Rahim's servant leadership philosophy developed through his work in human services where he served the needs of inner-city families and at-risk children for over 15 years. The same servant leadership approach that made him successful in human services also contributed to his achievements as a corporate executive and academic officer. Recognized as a 2014 Empact100 Honoree by the United Nations in NYC for my social entrepreneurship work, and participated in the Empact Entrepreneurship Summit, an invite-only event hosted at the White House and U.S. Chamber of Commerce in Washington DC. He received the 2011 Certified Manager of the Year Award from ICPM at James Madison University, 2010 Entrepreneurship Teaching Excellence Award from Oklahoma State University, and was a Finalist for the 2010 CEC Educator of Year Award.

Dr. Rahim currently serves as the Kotouc Endowed Chair at Bellevue University and JWMI Fellow at the Jack Welch Management Institute. His story was turned into a short documentary and adapted into a theater production titled 'Tales from the Salt City,' written by celebrated playwright and award-winning director, Ping Chong. He has been featured in the Huffington Post, Forbes Magazine and CEO Magazine. He also appeared in a national advertisement campaign and have been interviewed on the BBC, NPR, PBS and other radio and podcast shows.

Dr. Rahim completed his Post-Doctoral studies at Harvard University, Tulane University and the University of Maryland/UC. He earned a Doctorate in Management, and two graduate degrees in business from Colorado Technical University, and completed his undergraduate education at SUNY Empire State College. He was the former University Dean at Colorado Tech, Curriculum Dean at Strayer University, and served as the Entrepreneur-in-Residence at Oklahoma State University.